Mark Hancock's 50 Tips for Teaching Pronunciation

T0275207

Cambridge Handbooks for Language Teachers

This series, now with over 50 titles, offers practical ideas, techniques and activities for the teaching of English and other languages, providing inspiration for both teachers and trainers.

The Pocket Editions come in a handy, pocket-sized format and are crammed full of tips and ideas from experienced English language teaching professionals, to enrich your teaching practice.

Recent titles in this series:

Grammar Practice Activities (Second edition)
A practical guide for teachers
PENNY UR

Vocabulary Activities
PENNY UR

Classroom Management Techniques
JIM SCRIVENER

CLIL Activities
A resource for subject and language teachers
LIZ DALE AND ROSIE TANNER

Language Learning with Technology
Ideas for integrating technology in the classroom
GRAHAM STANLEY

Translation and Own-language Activities
PHILIP KERR

Language Learning with Digital Video
BEN GOLDSTEIN AND PAUL DRIVER

Discussions and More
Oral fluency practice in the classroom
PENNY UR

Interaction Online
Creative Activities for Blended Learning
LINDSAY CLANDFIELD AND JILL HADFIELD

Activities for Very Young Learners
HERBERT PUCHTA AND KAREN ELLIOTT

Recent Pocket Editions:

Penny Ur's 100 Teaching Tips
PENNY UR

Jack C. Richards' 50 Tips for Teacher Development
JACK C. RICHARDS

Scott Thornbury's 30 Language Teaching Methods
SCOTT THORNBURY

Alan Maley's 50 Creative Activities
ALAN MALEY

Scott Thornbury's 101 Grammar Questions
SCOTT THORNBURY

Carol Read's 50 Tips for Teaching Primary Children
CAROL READ

David Crystal's 50 Questions About English Usage
DAVID CRYSTAL

Mark Hancock's 50 Tips for Teaching Pronunciation

Mark Hancock

Consultant and editor: Scott Thornbury

CAMBRIDGE
UNIVERSITY PRESS

CAMBRIDGE
UNIVERSITY PRESS

University Printing House, Cambridge CB2 8BS, United Kingdom

One Liberty Plaza, 20th Floor, New York, NY 10006, USA

477 Williamstown Road, Port Melbourne, VIC 3207, Australia

314–321, 3rd Floor, Plot 3, Splendor Forum, Jasola District Centre, New Delhi – 110025, India

79 Anson Road, #06–04/06, Singapore 079906

Cambridge University Press is part of the University of Cambridge.

It furthers the University's mission by disseminating knowledge in the pursuit of education, learning and research at the highest international levels of excellence.

www.cambridge.org
Information on this title: www.cambridge.org/9781108744966

© Cambridge University Press 2020

First published 2020

20 19 18 17 16 15 14 13 12 11 10 9 8 7 6 5 4 3 2 1

Printed in Great Britain by Ashford Colour Press Ltd.

A catalogue record for this publication is available from the British Library

ISBN 978-1-108-74496-6 Paperback
ISBN 978-1-108-74500-0 Apple iBook
ISBN 978-1-108-74498-0 Google ebook
ISBN 978-1-108-74499-7 Kindle ebook
ISBN 978-1-108-74497-3 eBooks.com ebook

Contents

Integrating pronunciation

How to teach pronunciation

Presentation

Practice

Feedback and assessment

Resources

Thanks

I would like to thank Scott Thornbury for the initial impulse that got me started on this book, as well as his wise editorial advice. Thanks also to Jo Timerick at Cambridge University Press for guiding the project and to Alison Sharpe for her careful editing of the various drafts of the manuscript.

Acknowledgements

The authors and publishers acknowledge the following sources of copyright material and are grateful for the permissions granted. While every effort has been made, it has not always been possible to identify the sources of all the material used, or to trace all copyright holders. If any omissions are brought to our notice, we will be happy to include the appropriate acknowledgements on reprinting and in the next update to the digital edition, as applicable.

Key: C = Chapter

Text

C40: Text taken from 'M is for Minimal pairs: Video' by Scott Thornbury, An A-Z of ELT https://scottthornbury.wordpress.com/. Reproduced with kind permission of Scott Thornbury; **C43:** Text taken from *PronPack 4: Pronunciation Poems* by Mark Hancock and Amanda Hancock, Vol 4. Copyright © 2017 Hancock McDonald ELT. Reproduced with kind permission of Mark Hancock and Amanda Hancock; **C50:** Chart taken from 'The Charts - The UK Chart' by Adrian Underhill. The Original Sound Foundations Phonemic Chart. Copyright © 2008 Adrian Underhill. Published by Macmillan Education. Reproduced with permission of Adrian Underhill; **C50:** Chart taken from *PronPack 1: Pronunciation Workouts* by Mark Hancock and Amanda Hancock, Vol 1. Copyright © 2017 Hancock McDonald ELT. Design: Amanda Hancock. Reproduced with kind permission of Mark Hancock and Amanda Hancock.

URLs

The publisher has used its best endeavours to ensure that the URLs for external websites referred to in this book are correct and active at the time of going to press. However, the publisher has no responsibility for the websites and can make no guarantee that a site will remain live or that the content is or will remain appropriate.

Why I wrote this book

I wrote this book for teachers of English who feel the need for guidance in dealing with pronunciation. Although learners usually place pronunciation high up on their list of priorities, it is often neglected by teachers, perhaps because it seems difficult to teach. I'm hoping that this book will convince readers that pronunciation teaching need not be 'difficult', and that it can in fact be a pleasure. Could pronunciation be the part of the lesson that you and your learners look forward to most? *I* think so!

The reader I have in mind is a general English teacher, rather than a specialist. By 'specialist', I mean, for example, somebody teaching phonology on a linguistics course, or somebody who is training air-traffic controllers. By 'general English teacher', I mean somebody whose learners will need their English for general international communication, rather than some very specific professional or personal purpose.

The reader may not have a specific interest in **phonology**, beyond the basics they need in order to teach. For that reason, I have tried to keep the tips as light as possible in terms of terminology. I see no reason to put obstacles in the path of those who would seek to explore this fascinating area of language teaching. Where I *have* introduced a technical term, it is printed in bold (see 'phonology' above) and you will find a brief explanation of it in the glossary.

I imagine the reader may well be looking for practical advice on a wide range of issues, rather than in-depth analysis of one specific area. I have tried to strike a balance between 'zooming in' to focus on details, and 'zooming out' to get a wide view of the subject as a whole. I think this balance of detail and big picture is important, so that we don't focus exclusively on one thing and neglect the rest.

I wrote this book in the form of fifty standalone tips. You may choose to go through them in sequence from beginning to end, or simply to dip in to the topic that is of interest at any given moment. Each tip has references to useful teaching resources and further reading on the aspect of pronunciation focused on in the tip. The order of the content is not random. The tips are grouped into three sections A–C, and I would like to explain the rationale behind this.

I think that pronunciation teachers need to answer three big questions before going into the classroom: why, what and how. 'Why' refers to the reason your learners need to develop their pronunciation – their purpose. 'What' refers to the content that you are teaching them – the phonology. 'How' refers to the materials and techniques that you use to teach it – the pedagogy. I think each of these questions is equally important and for a balanced approach, we need to consider all three. Think of a table with three legs: if you remove one, the table falls over! The three sections of this book correspond to the three questions: A. Goals and models; B. What to teach; C. How to teach it.

For readers wishing to go into more detail about any of the three questions, I would suggest the following books, in addition to the ones that are referenced in some of the tips:

Why (purpose)

Jenkins, J. (2000) *The Phonology of English as an International Language.* Oxford: Oxford University Press.

Levis, J. (2018) *Intelligibility, Oral Communication, and the Teaching of Pronunciation.* Cambridge: Cambridge University Press.

Walker, R. (2010) *Teaching the Pronunciation of English as a Lingua Franca.* Oxford: Oxford University Press.

What (phonology)

Catford, J. C. (2001) *A Practical Introduction to Phonetics.* Oxford: Oxford University Press.

Cruttenden, A. (2014) *Gimson's Pronunciation of English.* Oxford: Routledge.

Roach, P. (2000) *English Phonetics and Phonology.* Cambridge: Cambridge University Press.

How (pedagogy)

Celce-Murcia, M., Brinton, D. M. and Goodwin, J. M. (2010) *Teaching Pronunciation.* Cambridge: Cambridge University Press.

Derwing, T. M. and Munro, M. J. (2015) *Pronunciation Fundamentals.* Amsterdam: John Benjamins.

Underhill, A. (2005) *Sound Foundations.* Oxford: Macmillan.

And for actual teaching materials, there are the books below:

Gilbert, J. B. (2012) *Clear Speech*. Cambridge: Cambridge University Press.

Hancock, M. (2017) *English Pronunciation in Use Intermediate*. Cambridge: Cambridge University Press.

Hewings, M. (2017) *English Pronunciation in Use Advanced*. Cambridge: Cambridge University Press.

Marks, J. (2017) *English Pronunciation in Use Elementary*. Cambridge: Cambridge University Press.

A: Goals and models

The tips in this section are concerned with the purposes of pronunciation teaching. Here, we deal with such issues as accent and intelligibility, learner motivation and English as a Lingua Franca.

Keep your eye on the goal
1 Focus on intelligibility
2 Be coherent about outcomes
3 Don't obsess about target models

Focus on the learners
4 Discuss the class objectives
5 Find out what motivates learners
6 Find out about your learners' L1
7 Be aware of factors that can affect the learners' pronunciation

Focus on the context
8 Raise awareness of English as a Lingua Franca
9 Identify priorities
10 Focus on accommodation skills
11 Identify any special purposes

Focus on the teacher
12 Don't worry that your accent is non-standard
13 Be aware of your own accent

1 Focus on intelligibility

Teaching pronunciation is about helping your learners
to become more intelligible in the target language. It's
important to regularly check that what you are doing in
class contributes to this basic objective.

In many languages, there are **accents** which are thought to be elegant
and others which are felt to be ugly. Speakers with an elegant accent
are perceived to be better educated and more intelligent than speakers
with an ugly accent. Consequently, to improve their prospects in life,
speakers may attempt to 'improve' their accent through **elocution**
lessons. I write 'improve' in quotes, because this evaluation is based on
prejudice rather than any intrinsic superiority of the prestige accent.

I am often surprised by how many teachers and learners seem to
think pronunciation classes are essentially the same thing as elocution
lessons – helping the learner to acquire a 'better' accent (again, I put
quotes around the evaluative word). To me, the purpose of learning a
language is to communicate – to understand and be understood. In this
context, pronunciation is less about sounding good and more about
being intelligible.

I feel this insight is so fundamental that it deserves to be the first tip
in this book: when you are teaching pronunciation, always check
that in the end, you are focusing on intelligibility. Whether you are
presenting a pronunciation point or giving a learner feedback on their
pronunciation, always keep this question in mind: *Why am I doing this?*
Your answer may be one of these:

- This will help my learner to be more clearly understood.
- This will help my learner to understand other speakers more easily.

In this case, you know you are on the right path because there is a good
reason for doing what you are doing; you aren't simply teaching a
pronunciation point because it exists.

If you teach in a context where the classes come from mixed linguistic backgrounds, it is relatively easy to tell what is intelligible and what is not. A Japanese learner, for example, may misunderstand a Mexican classmate because of a certain **vowel** sound. A German learner may misunderstand a Vietnamese classmate because of a stress pattern. The problems stand out, not only to the teacher, but also to the learners themselves.

However, intelligibility is less easy to judge in a context where most of the class have the same language background. In this context, the learners will tend to settle on a form of pronunciation which is intelligible amongst themselves but may be unintelligible to outsiders. The problem can be compounded when the teacher also shares the same language background, or has spent so long with learners from that language background that he or she no longer notices the local idiosyncrasies.

If you work in a context where your learners share the same **L1**, it is a good idea to regularly refresh your memory about which localised pronunciation features are non-problematic and which ones are likely to lead to misunderstandings. If you share the same L1 as your learners, you will be in a good position to do this because you will be able to reflect on the communication problems you had when you were learning the **target language** yourself.

Intelligibility isn't such a simple concept as it seems at first sight, and you will probably need to revisit and refine your intuitions about what is intelligible during your teaching career. Keep in mind, too, that intelligibility is not just a question of language – it is *people* who are intelligible, not accents. Making yourself understood is not just a matter of your pronunciation – you also need to be flexible in interaction.

However, keeping the fundamental goal of intelligibility in mind whenever you teach pronunciation is a good place to start.

Levis, J. (2018) *Intelligibility, Oral Communication, and the Teaching of Pronunciation.* Cambridge: Cambridge University Press.

2 Be coherent about outcomes

> If our aim is intelligibility, then success is when the learners have achieved intelligible pronunciation. To be intelligible, it is not necessary to sound like a native.

While almost everyone learns to pronounce their first language (L1) 'perfectly', the same is not true for their second language (L2). Here, the outcome is strongly dependent on the age that a person starts learning the L2: the older the learner, the less likely they are to acquire a 'native-like' **accent**. Once passed the age of puberty, very few will do so. This observation appears at first glance to offer little ground for optimism as regards pronunciation teaching and learning. However, I would argue that any such pessimism is misplaced.

The clues lie in the words I placed in quotation marks above: 'perfectly' and 'native-like'. They imply that the goal of pronunciation learning is to acquire a specific accent and any other accent would be less than perfect. However, what if this is not the goal? What if the goal is not to acquire a certain accent, but rather to become a clearly intelligible L2 speaker? It is perfectly possible for a learner to achieve this outcome *without* sounding like a native. Of all of the possible accents of English, there is no evidence that the native ones are necessarily more intelligible globally.

Given the goal of pronunciation learning is intelligibility, we need to be coherent about outcomes. If we agree that the desired outcome is intelligibility, we should not then judge our learners' success in terms of how 'native-like' their pronunciation is. Instead, it should be judged in terms of how effective it is: is the learner able to make himself or herself understood? The presence of a noticeable L1-influenced accent need not be a handicap in this regard.

I should clarify that up to now, I have been talking about teaching pronunciation to non-specialist learners. We must bear in mind that there may be learners who need English for Specific Purposes (ESP), and in some cases, this may have implications for pronunciation goals. For example, you may be teaching a class of learners who are preparing for a professional role that requires them to acquire a specific native accent, or something as close to that as possible. This may be the case for would-be call centre staff, for example (see Tip 11). We could describe our endeavour in such circumstances as teaching 'Pronunciation for Specific Purposes' or perhaps 'accent training', and in this realm, the criteria for success would be entirely different. However, this book is not about accent training.

We must also bear in mind that our learners may themselves not be clear about their desired outcomes. Naturally enough, most of them will not have been trained in applied linguistics, and their view may reflect what is taken to be common sense to society at large. If you ask the average person in the street, they may say it's obvious that the objective of learning to speak, say, Italian is 'to sound like an Italian'. It would take a bit more focused thought to refine that objective to something like 'to make myself understood in Italian'. As pronunciation teachers, we may need to devote some class time to negotiating and refining objectives in this way.

One simple tip in this regard would be: present L1-appropriate potential role-models. For example, for a Thai learner of English, a role-model could be a well-known Thai person who speaks English in a way which is widely intelligible, rather than, say, a British or American celebrity. You could play a selection of short videos of local celebrities speaking English to initiate a discussion about pronunciation goals.

Derwing, T. M. and Munro, M. J. (2015) *Pronunciation Fundamentals*. Amsterdam: John Benjamins.

3 Don't obsess about target models

> The choice of target model is probably not as important as people sometimes believe. Intelligibility does not depend on the learners sounding exactly like any specific model. In any case, as the teacher, the main model is you!

Let's say a footballer aims for the centre of the net but the ball goes into the corner of it instead. Is this a success or a failure? A success, surely – a goal is a goal, after all. Similarly, in pronunciation learning, I think the goal is much wider than the specific point you may be aiming at. For instance, you may aim at a standard British or American English, but succeed in producing perfectly intelligible English that *isn't* obviously British or American. Congratulations – you've scored!

I mentioned British and American as targets because these are perhaps the models we see most widely offered. There may of course be others, such as Australian or Scottish, but in my view we needn't make a big issue about the choice of target. All of them are well between the posts of the same goal, and in the end, the learner will probably hit the back of the net in a slightly different spot anyway, typically by producing a version of English which is **L1**-flavoured.

At this point, it may be worth making a distinction between a reference model and an attainment standard. To return to the football metaphor, the reference model is the precise point the learner aims at. The attainment standard is the entire goal, and the learner may happily settle for any shot which results in the ball going in. I suspect that the reference model is sometimes mistaken for an attainment standard, such that any deviation from it is seen as 'incorrect'. The consequences of this seem absurd. Let me explain.

Reference models of English pronunciation are what we typically find in dictionaries and other published material. For British English, for example, the reference model may be what is known as Received

Pronunciation (**RP**), while for American it may be General American (**GA**). I personally speak a version of British English which differs in some respects from RP. If we took the reference model to be an arbiter of correctness, I would have to confess to being in error, as indeed would the majority of British speakers. Can this be right?

As the title of this tip suggests, I think some people may obsess unnecessarily about which target model to choose. In some cases, it may be an obsession which is fuelled by commercial interests: schools may offer learners a specific **accent** such as 'British English' in the belief that this is a selling point. Learners see 'British English' being offered by a number of schools and conclude that it must be desirable. In this way, the advert creates a demand for the thing it is advertising.

However, offering learners a choice of target accents as if they were outfits in a clothing store seems unrealistic in the extreme. To begin with, as I have said, the learner is unlikely to come out speaking with exactly the accent selected. Then there is the teacher's accent. Few teachers can just change their accents at will, according to the stated preference of the learner. Realistically, teachers will teach in their own accent, whatever that may be.

We could sum up the situation as follows. The learners in your class are subjected to a variety of influences:

- you, the teacher, with whatever accent you have

- the reference models presented in the various materials you use

- the various forms of English that the learner is exposed to outside the classroom

- the learner's own background – especially their L1 (see Tip 6)

- last but not least, the learner's own interests and motives – celebrities who they would like to sound like, for example.

With all of these things going on, do we really need to obsess about target models?

4   Discuss the class objectives

> Learners sometimes have unrealistic ideas about the aims of working on their pronunciation. You may need to spend some class time talking about accents and the idea of 'correctness'.

Of all possible shades of blue, which one is the bluest? It's strangely tempting to think that this question makes sense. Many of us might feel we could, if necessary, select the bluest blue from a number of samples. There may even be a degree of consensus between us. However, the question is essentially subjective.

A similar question could be asked of **accents** – which one is the purest, or most correct? I've been told, for example, that the purest accent of Spanish is to be heard in the city of Valladolid. Other people have told me that it's in Burgos. Learners who believe that there is such a thing as a purest accent may assume that there must be one for English too, and without question, this is the one they should master. In the realm of British English, for example, I've heard mention of 'Oxford English', or 'the Queen's English'. Clearly, unless you share this view of pronunciation, there may be a need to negotiate the class objectives with such learners.

There is no doubt that as regards teaching pronunciation, English is a special case amongst languages, in that it is probably the most international language. The majority of learners globally are likely to use it as a Lingua Franca (**ELF**), often with other non-native speakers. You may find that this fact is worth pointing out to your class. You may even feel the need to go into the issue in greater depth. The book referenced at the end of this tip has 14 different lesson plans for discussing issues relating to ELF with learners, so clearly the authors perceive a need (see Tip 8).

I would say that at the very least, you need to make sure your learners appreciate the following three points:

1   No matter how 'standard' your own accent is, you cannot guarantee that the people you speak with will also have that accent. Even

if you travel to a country where English is spoken as a native language, you will hear a wide range of accents, both native and non-native. You therefore need to be able to deal with 'non-standard' pronunciation receptively at least.

2   Even if you speak with a 'standard' accent, you cannot guarantee that the people you speak with will understand you easily – 'standard' accents are not necessarily more intelligible than other accents, globally. You may therefore need to modify the way you speak in order to make yourself understood even if you speak the standard accent perfectly.

3   Although you may choose a 'standard' accent as a target to aim for, you should bear in mind that not many learners actually hit that precise target. Most learners end up speaking with an accent which is recognisably different from the 'standard' one. However, this is not necessarily a problem for intelligibility.

None of the points mentioned above should prevent your learners from striving for a 'standard' accent if they feel so inclined, or if they feel it would benefit them in their future circumstances. If they insist that this is their goal, you can take account of it in the way you provide feedback to them on their pronunciation.

Finally, you may of course find that you need to encourage learners in the other direction: there are some who feel that pronunciation doesn't matter and that 'anything goes'. Such learners may benefit from feedback such as the following:

- 'If you pronounce it that way, you are almost certainly going to be misunderstood. I strongly advise you to work on this.'
- 'I understand you if you pronounce it that way, but you may find some people don't. If the person you're speaking to clearly doesn't understand, you may have to pronounce it differently.'
- 'Many people, including native speakers, pronounce it the way you do. However, it is not "standard", and you might find that some people disapprove of it. You should probably avoid it, especially in formal contexts.'

Kiczkowiak, M. and Lowe, R. J. (2018) *Teaching English as a Lingua Franca.* Peaslake: Delta Publishing.

5 Find out what motivates learners

> Learners may have an intrinsic interest in the language they are learning, or they may simply need it for practical reasons. This will affect their motivation. You can also enhance motivation by what you do in class. Try to find out your learners' reasons for learning and their preferred class activities.

Two of my language learning experiences have been with Portuguese and Spanish, and on reflection, I see that I was motivated differently in either case. For Portuguese, I really loved the sound of the language, perhaps because I was a great fan of popular Brazilian music, and I really wanted to speak like a Carioca. Some years later, I started learning Spanish without any such drive. Initially, I just needed to make myself understood reasonably well, but I wasn't too worried about sounding like a native.

My Portuguese experience was an example of *integrative* motivation, in which the learner is specifically attracted by the culture associated with the target language. My Spanish experience, by contrast, was an example of *instrumental* motivation, where the learner needs to speak the language for a practical purpose. This may be making themselves understood in a country where the language is spoken or improving their career prospects or passing an exam.

The fact that English is so widespread, and that learning it is obligatory in many educational contexts, probably means that most learners have a more instrumental motivation. However, many may also have interests which give them a degree of integrative motivation too. For the pronunciation teacher, it is worth finding out about these needs and interests and taking them into account. For example, learners planning to use English for travel will probably be motivated by functional language role-plays. Learners planning to interact online with other people who share the same interest may enjoy digital activities. For learners interested in English medium movies and music, lyrics and video may be motivating.

Although you, the teacher, can work with the learners' integrative and instrumental motivations, you have no control over them. There are other aspects of motivation, however, that you can enhance or otherwise by what you do in class. For example, for more fun-loving learners, you can use playful activities – see, for example, my book *Pronunciation Games*. For more 'cerebral' learners, you can use problem-solving activities. This is true for any aspect of language teaching, be it grammar, vocabulary or skills work. However, there is one aspect of motivation which is specifically relevant to pronunciation, and that is your learners' attitude to risk.

As a teacher, you need to notice the following about your learners: do they hate sounding stupid in front of their classmates or are they happy to risk making mistakes? This relates to the concept of 'face', which is something like dignity or social prestige. The fact is that trying to pronounce a new language in public is a threat to a person's 'face' – it exposes them to ridicule. Some learners feel this 'threat' so strongly that it may damage their motivation in the pronunciation class, and teachers need to be aware of this.

It is good to use activities that will suit both the risk-takers and risk-avoiders in your class. A good example of this is choral drilling: you model the chunk of language you are focusing on and the class repeats it after you, all together. Some will speak out loud, others may mumble quietly; still others may be silent, but perhaps repeating in their mind. Whichever they choose to do, there is benefit in it, but no threatening exposure.

Given that most classes will have a mix of learners with a mix of motivations and preferences, the best approach is perhaps to try different things out and observe. Don't assume that they'll hate this or that activity: give it a try – you may be surprised. If you don't know what will motivate them, this is how you will find out!

Hancock, M. (1995) *Pronunciation Games*. Cambridge: Cambridge University Press.

6 Find out about your learners' L1

> It is a big advantage for pronunciation teachers to know their learners' L1. If you don't, it's worth finding out as much as you can. You can ask your learners about their own language(s) if necessary.

Teaching pronunciation when you know nothing of your learners' L1 is like wading across a river when you can't see what's under the water. It can be difficult and inefficient: sometimes you put too much emphasis on a point that the learners get easily, other times you pass too quickly over a point that the learners have great difficulty with. We look at this issue in two contexts – monolingual and multilingual classes.

Scenario 1: Monolingual classes

The learners are studying in a school in their home country. The learners share the same L1. If you also share this language, you already know about your learners' L1 of course, but you may not be taking full advantage of this fact in your pronunciation teaching. The reason for this may be that while you studied the **phonology** of the target language during your studies and training, you may never have studied the phonology of your own mother tongue. If you don't share the same language as your learners, see the tips below in Scenario 2.

One benefit of having a detailed knowledge of the L1 pronunciation is that you may find that it has unsuspected similarities with the **target language**. For example, there may be a **phoneme** in English which is not a phoneme in the L1 but *does* occur in certain specific circumstances. Robin Walker provides the following examples from Spanish:

- While /z/ is not a phoneme in Spanish, the sound does occur in certain contexts, for example between the 'e' and the 'd' in *desde* (since).
- While /ʃ/ is not a phoneme in Spanish, the sound does occur in certain **accents**, for example, the 'ch' in *muchacho* (young man) in an Andalusian accent.

If learners are having difficulty with /z/ or /ʃ/, it can help if you point out these sounds when they occur in the L1. Robin Walker's book (see below) contains a reference section for such sound coincidences with English, for 10 different languages.

Scenario 2: Multilingual classes

The learners are studying in a country where the target language is spoken, and they share the class with other learners from different language backgrounds. You, the teacher, do not speak all these languages yourself – and possibly none of them.

One thing you can do if you are teaching in this scenario is some background reading on the L1s of your learners. A useful reference here is the book *Learner English* by Swan and Smith (see below). You may also find helpful notes through internet searches.

Another thing you can do is try to find out as much as possible from the learners themselves. Here are some examples of the kinds of questions I have found myself asking in one way or another:

1 Are there a lot of different **accents** in your language?
2 Is there one accent which is thought to be more 'correct'?
3 Are learners taught about the pronunciation of your language at school?
4 Are there any sounds in your native language that some people find hard to learn?
5 Is the pronunciation of your language reflected in the written form?
6 How many **vowel** sounds are there?
7 Does your language have long and short vowel sounds?
8 Do most words end with a vowel?
9 Do any words have two or more **consonant** sounds together?
10 Do you have a contrast between strong and weak syllables in your language?
11 Are there any sounds which never occur at the end of a word?
12 Are there any sounds which never occur next to each other?
13 In your language, can a different **tone** change the meaning of a word?

Swan, M. and Smith, B. (2001) *Learner English*. Cambridge: Cambridge University Press.

Walker, R. (2010) *Teaching the Pronunciation of English as a Lingua Franca*. Oxford: Oxford University Press.

7 Be aware of factors that can affect the learners' pronunciation

Our learners' pronunciation problems are often a result of influence from their L1. However, there are various other factors which can affect their pronunciation and we need to keep an open mind.

Pronunciation teachers usually suffer from a certain professional bias, just as other professionals do. If a person walks into room, the hairdresser will see a head of hair, the dentist will see a set of teeth, and the tailor will see a type of body shape. And when the person starts to speak, the pronunciation teacher will hear a collection of **accent** features.

Among the factors that affect the learner's pronunciation, their L1 is probably the biggest, and it may be tempting to view this as the cause of all issues. However, it's wise to be on the alert for other explanations too. Remember that there may sometimes be other issues which aren't specifically about pronunciation. You can waste a lot of time when your diagnosis of the cause of a problem is wrong.

Another big factor is spelling. For example, pronouncing *bear* so that it sounds the same as *beer* is a typical learner error, and I suspect that usually, it has nothing to do with inability to produce the **vowel** sound in *bear*. It is almost certainly a problem caused by spelling: the learner has seen the 'ear' combination in words like *near*, *hear* and *ear* and has generalised the pronunciation of this letter sequence from these examples.

It's not only the spelling of the **target language** which may cause problems – L1 spellings may also interfere. For example, many Brazilian learners of English pronounce *rock* as *hock*, because the letter 'r' at the beginning of a word is pronounced like /h/ in their language. Often, the learner is well capable of pronouncing the /r/ but doesn't do so because of the spelling.

There is another aspect to the example of *rock* in Brazil. The English word is used as a loan word for the musical style in Portuguese, so that the learner is accustomed to saying it in their L1, following the L1 pronunciation rules. A similar example from Japanese is *rajio* for radio. There is a very strong temptation for learners to mispronounce loan words from English when speaking English: they have been saying these words for years, perhaps supposing that their L1 version is the correct English pronunciation.

Apart from linguistic factors such as L1 and spelling, there may be more sociological factors at work. As a pronunciation teacher, you need to keep in mind that some learners deliberately avoid some target language pronunciation features, wanting perhaps to preserve some of their native accent as a mark of their identity. In some classrooms, there is also peer pressure at work. For example, teenagers may resist adopting foreign sounds into their speech for fear of sounding ridiculous in front of their classmates, or being seen as the 'teacher's pet'.

Last but not least among the factors affecting pronunciation learning that we need to be aware of are physiological ones. I recently had a Russian learner in my class who pronounced /r/ in a strange, guttural way. I supposed that it was interference from the learner's L1, although it sounded more French than Russian to me. We spent some time working on that sound, but then the learner informed me that he had a speech problem and he had been unable to articulate /r/ since childhood. This was a possibility that I'd overlooked. Other physiological issues we need to bear in mind include learning difficulties such as dyslexia, or physical disabilities such as poor hearing. When diagnosing our learner's problems, we need to keep an open mind.

English differs from other languages in that it is a global Lingua Franca. Speaking English enables learners to communicate with people from anywhere in the world, not just Britain and the USA, for example. It is useful for learners to be aware of that fact.

If you are learning to speak Turkish, it is highly likely that you are doing so in order to make yourself understood in Turkey or with Turkish people. It's very unlikely that you would be learning it in preparation for a trip to Greece or Egypt. You may on the other hand be learning *English* in preparation for a trip to all three of those countries. That's because people nowadays use English as a Lingua Franca (ELF). For example, a Turk and a Greek may use English as a means of communication between themselves, even though neither of them is a native speaker of that language.

It seems obvious that the vast numbers of people learning English today cannot *all* be doing so with a view to living in or visiting an English-speaking country. It seems much more likely that most will use English as a Lingua Franca. Yet this reality is often ignored in the mindset of teachers and learners of the language. English language schools and classrooms, for example, are often adorned with iconic images and flags from Britain or the USA, and nobody seems to find that odd. Why a red telephone box? Why not a Chinese pagoda?

I suspect that this is a hangover from the past, when English was a foreign language like any other. The French classroom would have pictures of baguettes and the Eiffel Tower, the English classroom would have Big Ben and a nice pot of tea. Learners perhaps imagined themselves in the future being in those places and chatting fluently with the locals. While this image may be motivating for some, it will be irrelevant for others, and it may be worth updating the way we portray the English language to reflect its reality in today's world. To this end, we need to raise awareness of ELF.

The evolution of English to world Lingua Franca status has major implications for pronunciation teaching. As a Lingua Franca, English is no longer 'owned' by the people of any country – it is the 'property' of all. This means that no single country can set standards of correctness. Nobody has the right to judge whether somebody else's **accent** is acceptable or not. It no longer makes sense to talk about whether a form of pronunciation is 'correct' – what matters is whether it works.

How can we raise awareness of ELF in the pronunciation classroom? One possibility is simply to tell the learners about it. For example, talk about colonial history and how English expanded to become an international language. Explain that among English users in the world, the non-native speakers now vastly outnumber the natives. However, I think it may be better to lead by example rather than just telling learners facts. What I mean by that is to assume ELF naturally in your manner of speaking, and in the way you respond to what your learners say.

This will mean, for example, not talking about 'correctness', and instead focusing on intelligibility. It will mean avoiding expressions like: 'It's pronounced …', which assume a single correct possibility, and disguises *who* it is that says it that way. And it will mean speaking even-handedly about different world accents, both native and non-native, with no assumption of superiority for any one of them. Here are some examples of the kinds of things you might say:

- 'This is the pronunciation given in the dictionary, but you can also say it that way – people will understand you.'
- 'British speakers often use a **weak form** here, but you don't have to. It is not important for intelligibility.'
- 'American speakers pronounce the "r" like that, but Scottish and Spanish speakers usually say it like this.'

Seidlhofer, B. (2011) *Understanding English as a Lingua Franca*. Oxford: Oxford University Press.

Some features of pronunciation are essential for intelligibility, others are optional. We should teach the optional features for listening skills, and the essential features for both spoken production *and* listening.

Have you got a key handy? Take it out and have a look. You'll notice that it has two ends – the end which fits into the lock (we'll call this the business end), and the end which you hold (the handle). Now consider this question: which end is more important?

I think you'll agree that both ends are important, but in different ways. The business end does the job of opening the door, and the shape must be exactly right or it won't work. The handle is necessary because you need *something* to hold, but the exact shape doesn't matter – the key will still work even if the shape of the handle is different.

We can think of the key as a metaphor for pronunciation. At the 'business' end of pronunciation are those features which are *essential* for intelligibility, and the shape is important. At the 'handle' end are features which are *optional*: they are important if you want to sound 'native-like', but if your goal is simply to be intelligible then the exact shape doesn't matter. Here's an example of each:

Essential: The **phoneme** /p/ needs to be pronounced clearly enough so that the listener can distinguish it from other phonemes such as /b/ or /f/. If you don't do this, you are likely to be misunderstood.

Optional: The word *to* has a strong form /tuː/ and a **weak form** /tə/. The weak form is easier to articulate when you are speaking quickly so it can help your fluency. If you use it, you will sound more native-like, but if you don't use it, you will still be understood.

To me, it is obvious that essential features such as the phoneme /p/ should be given priority over optional features such as the weak form

/tə/, at least as regards the learner's *productive* skill. However, optional features may be important as regards their *receptive* skill. For example, although learners don't have to use weak forms in their own speech, they are likely to hear them in the speech of others, and as listeners, they will need to be able to understand them. So weak forms may be optional for speaking but essential for listening.

How are we to know which features of pronunciation are essential or optional? I think the key to this question is to think of the reason for the feature. Does it serve to make meaning clearer? Then it's essential. Does it serve to make speech easier to articulate? Then it's optional. The optional features are basically all of those which come under the umbrella term of 'connected speech'. These include **schwa**, **weak forms**, **elision**, **linking**, **intrusive sounds** and **assimilation**. When we teach these features, therefore, it is principally for the purpose of developing the learners' listening skills.

I think it's a reasonable starting point to consider the features of connected speech as optional and the remaining features as essential. However, if you want to go into more detail, you'll need to consider **accent** variation. I suggested above that making clear distinctions between phonemes is important, but some distinctions are missing in some accents. For example, many speakers in London and elsewhere do not distinguish /θ/ from /f/, and yet they are still widely understood. So perhaps /θ/ is less essential than /p/? Jennifer Jenkins conducted research which appears to back this up: it was found that failure to produce an accurate /θ/ was never the cause of misunderstanding. For this reason, she left /θ/ off her list of pronunciation features which are essential for intelligibility in the context of English as a Lingua Franca. The list is known as the '**Lingua Franca Core**', and it is worth looking at if you want further guidance in identifying priorities.

Jenkins, J. (2000) *The Phonology of English as an International Language.* Oxford: Oxford University Press.

10   Focus on accommodation skills

> Learners need to be flexible enough to adapt to the people they talk to. This will involve being tolerant of other accents (receptive accommodation) and being able to modify their own speech (productive accommodation).

Sometimes we teach pronunciation in a very one-sided way. We focus on nurturing the learners' spoken pronunciation skills without taking into account their future interlocutors. However, as the expression goes, 'it takes two to tango'. Your pronunciation can be as good as you like, but it won't be much use if you are unable to adapt to the person you're talking to. This skill of adapting to your interlocutor is known as *accommodation*.

In the book referenced at the end of this tip, Chia Suan Chong describes useful general accommodation skills in international communication. But here, I would like to focus more specifically on the role of *pronunciation* in these skills, and divide this into two parts – receptive and productive accommodation.

Receptive accommodation

I think that, traditionally, we had the idea that everyone would learn to speak in a standard **accent** such as Received Pronunciation (**RP**) or General American (**GA**), and they would in turn understand anybody else who also spoke with that same accent. However, any visitor to the US or the UK will have noticed that the people there don't always speak with the standard accent. And when we widen our focus to include English across the whole world, then this idea of a single standard is unrealistic in the extreme!

Learners – and their teachers too – need to be flexible enough to cope with accent variation. Consider the following sentence, which is written 'with an accent':

The ket set on the met.

A flexible listener will hear this sentence and, after some initial confusion, will understand that the speaker means, *The cat sat on the mat*, but in their accent, the *a* sounds like /e/. The listener will then adjust their expectation accordingly and from now on, they will understand the speaker more easily.

We can encourage such accent tolerance generally by making sure that we expose our learners to non-standard accents in the materials we use in class. In this way, they will get practice in 'adjusting their ear', as the listener did in the *cat* example above.

However, we can also take a more focused approach to **accent** variation. For example, the /r/ sound when it comes after a vowel (but not before one) is very vulnerable. In many accents, it disappears by being absorbed into the vowel before it, so that *court* sounds like *caught* for example. In other accents, it is always pronounced, so that *Karma* is different from *calmer*. Learners need to be aware of such an important accent variable, and I would always mention it when teaching /r/ or the vowel sounds which typically go before it. I would also make a point of allowing the learners to choose their preferred variant in their productive pronunciation.

Productive accommodation

We need to help learners to become aware of those features of their own speech which may lead to misunderstandings. Take for example the **vowel** contrast between /ɪ/ and /iː/. Many learners conflate these two sounds so that there is no difference between, for example, *fit* and *feet*. For some interlocutors, this may not be a problem, while others may sometimes be confused because of it. Learners who are aware that this may be an issue will be better able to adjust their own pronunciation as necessary.

People who speak English as their **L1** also need to adjust their pronunciation for the benefit of interlocutors. For example, there are features of connected speech which can make them *less* intelligible for some listeners. Use of **elision** and **weak forms** can mean that the words *a*, *are*, *her*, *of* and *or* all sound exactly the same, for instance. Obviously, this may be confusing for some listeners. Native speakers, and speakers who have acquired a native-like accent, need to be aware of such features in order to be able to accommodate more effectively.

Suan Chong, C. (2018) *Successful International Communication*. Hove: Pavillion Publishing.

Identify any special purposes

Some learners have special purposes beyond simply being more intelligible. These purposes may be professional, academic or personal in nature, and they may have implications for what we teach.

I think it is reasonable to regard intelligibility as the main goal of pronunciation learning (see Tip 1). However, we must also keep in mind the possibility that our learners have a special purpose beyond that. For example, some may be planning to emigrate to an English-speaking country. Clearly, if your learner is going to live in Singapore or Sydney or San Francisco, there will be implications for their pronunciation goals.

We could divide special purposes into three categories: professional, academic or personal. For each of these three, we will look at examples which may have an impact on what we teach in our pronunciation classes.

Professional

If your learners are preparing for jobs which involve dealing directly with clients, and if those clients happen to be native English speakers, then the learners will probably need to work more on acquiring a native-like **accent**. This need may be more acute if the 'clients' are people unaccustomed to international communication – many patients in UK hospitals may fall into this category, for example. Call centre workers too sometimes have to deal with rather unaccommodating clients.

A more native-like accent may also be required by learners who are aiming to work for a company which, for some reason, believes that a native accent has more prestige.

Finally, I should also mention professions which have specialist pronunciation needs, although these probably fall outside the remit of general pronunciation teaching. Examples include air-traffic controllers, or actors who need accent training.

Academic

Some English language exams have pronunciation grading criteria which go beyond what is strictly necessary for intelligibility. If your learners are preparing for such an exam, this will have implications on what you choose to focus on. Also, university students may have special needs such as presenting an academic paper. Such students will benefit from working on their reading aloud skills, for example.

Then there are learners who are studying English **phonology** as a subject and not just as a means of communication. They may be future language teachers, for example. Clearly, they will need to know more detail and metalanguage than general language learners. It's worth pointing out to trainee language teachers, however, that they need not inflict all of this detail on their future learners!

Personal

I mentioned above the special needs of people who are migrating to an English-speaking country. Immigrants in the USA, for example, often choose to attend **accent reduction** courses after finding that people respond badly to hearing their L1-influenced accent. It's sad but true that accent prejudice exists (see the reference below), and some learners may need help in reducing their chances of becoming a target for it.

Last but not least I would mention personal motivations. Some learners simply like a certain accent or feel motivated by a vision of themselves speaking English 'like a native'. We should respect their wishes in this.

Moyer, A. (2013) *Foreign Accent: The Phenomenon of Non-Native Speech*. Cambridge: Cambridge University Press.

12 Don't worry that your accent is non-standard

> For a pronunciation teacher, it is important to have an accent which is widely understood. It doesn't have to be a standard accent – standard accents are not necessarily more intelligible than other accents.

I have heard English teachers say things like, 'I don't teach pronunciation because I'm Scottish'. On the face of it, this seems almost as absurd as saying, 'I don't teach grammar because I'm blonde'. However, if we take into account assumptions which are often made about language instruction, the Scottish teacher's viewpoint makes more sense. One such assumption is that the goal of pronunciation teaching is to train the learner to speak like the model in the coursebook. For British English, this is likely to be Received Pronunciation (**RP**). For American English, it will probably be General American (**GA**). But what happens if you don't speak one of these standard **accents** yourself?

If you have this 'problem', then remember this: you are in the majority. Of all the English teachers in the world, only a small minority speak RP or GA. Does this mean that the majority of teachers are not qualified to teach pronunciation? Obviously not! So in that case, there must be something wrong with the assumption. In order to see what it is, we need to break it down into two parts, and deal with these in turn:

1 Learners will speak with the same accent as their teachers.
2 If my coursebook presents a standard accent, it must be because this is better than other accents.

1 Learners rarely leave their course of language classes sounding exactly like their teachers. The pronunciation they are exposed to in the class is only one factor in the accent they develop. There are other factors, and perhaps the strongest will be the influence of their first language. Teachers need not worry that everything they say will

be recorded and 'played back' to them through the mouths of their students! But even if learners do pick up their teacher's accent, that is not necessarily a bad thing, as we will see next.

2 Pronunciation coursebooks tend to present standard accents because they have to present *something* in their recordings and **phonemic** transcriptions. But this doesn't mean that the standard accent is better than, say, the teacher's accent. A standard accent may enjoy prestige in the country where it is spoken, but this is a result of social attitudes in that country rather than any intrinsic quality of the accent itself. So, for example, the fact that RP enjoys prestige in England does not mean that it is any more intelligible globally than a Scottish or Spanish accent. In many contexts, it may even be *less* intelligible.

So far, we have been discussing people's accents as if they only have a single fixed one. However, it is often the case that people have a repertoire of at least two accents and they can move between them according to context. So for example, our Scottish teacher may have an accent from, for example, an area of Glasgow, which they speak when at home among family and friends, and another accent which they use in more formal contexts or while away in other parts of the world. This second accent may be still Scottish but less local and more widely intelligible. It goes without saying that this accent will be the more suitable for the language class.

The situation is different for teachers who are not native speakers of the language they are teaching. For example, our Spanish teacher of English may not have a range of English accents to choose between. However, the same principle holds: if they are teaching English, they should aim to avoid speaking in a way which is only likely to be understood locally – in this case, to people familiar with Spanish.

To sum up, you shouldn't worry that your accent is non-standard, but you should try to be as intelligible as possible. If in doubt about how to achieve this, focus on those features of your accent which you know are most regional or L1-influenced and try to make those features less prominent (see Tip 13).

13 Be aware of your own accent

It's useful to be aware of your accent, not only in English, but also in your L1 (if that is not English). This will make you better able to raise your learners' awareness of accent variation, both in the target language and in their mother tongue.

'To know yourself is the beginning of wisdom'. These are words attributed to the ancient Greek philosopher Socrates. For the purposes of pronunciation learning and teaching, we could say the same, but change 'know' to 'hear'.

My first experience of 'hearing' myself was as a child. I was surprised to discover that some people pronounce 'laugh' with a long **vowel**, so that it rhymes with 'half'. For me, it had always had a short vowel so that it rhymed with 'gaffe'. I thought their pronunciation was weird. The 'beginning of wisdom' moment came next: I discovered that the feeling was mutual – the long-vowel people thought *I* sounded weird.

We pronunciation teachers are in the business of noticing how people sound when they speak, and what better place to start than with ourselves? It's always interesting, and often surprising, to make a recording of yourself speaking. First, you have to get used to the fact that your own voice sounds completely different when you are not hearing it coming from your own mouth. Then you can get down to the business of analysing your own **accent**: ask yourself questions such as these:

- Is there anything in my accent which reveals where I came from? How does it differ from other regional accents?
- Would somebody listening to me be able to guess my level of education, my profession or my social class? How?
- Do I have any personal idiosyncrasies in my pronunciation? What?
- Are there any influences from other languages in my accent? Which?

- Are there any features of my accent which could make me difficult to understand for some listeners? What features?

Awareness of your own accent is useful to have on a general level. But it also has more specific benefits if your own language is the one that the class is learning (**target language**), or if your own language is the same as your learners' mother tongue (**L1**). We will look at each of these possibilities in turn.

1 If you are a native speaker of the target language

If there are features of your own accent which might make you hard to understand, you could try and modify your speech when you are teaching the language. These features might include accent features which are not widely recognised outside your home region. They might also be features of fast connected speech which you use in relaxed, informal settings but which international listeners would find hard to decode.

Since you, as the teacher, are probably the target model that your learners will have most exposure to, you should make them aware of features of your pronunciation which are accent-specific, and which may be very different in other accents. For example, I might explain, 'In my accent, "laugh" rhymes with the first syllable of "café", but in the South of England it rhymes with "half".

2 You share the same L1 as your learners

You can use your awareness of accent variation in your own language to help learners. For example, if your learners are struggling with a sound in English, you can use examples from another accent of their L1 which resemble that sound (see Tip 6). You can also warn your class about which features of their L1 pronunciation may interfere with their English pronunciation in a way which damages intelligibility.

Finally, if you are teaching English and it's not your mother tongue, it may be worth recording yourself in English, and then listening to the recording and answering the questions above again.

B: What to Teach

The tips in this section are concerned with the content of what we teach in pronunciation classes – the phonology of English. We deal here with issues such as whether and how to use phonemic symbols, what to do about accent variation, and what aspects of connected speech and intonation to cover.

Don't teach pronunciation points 'because they exist', teach them because they are useful. Don't try to solve a pronunciation problem if your learners don't have that problem.

When you're choosing a pronunciation point to present to your class, think in terms of problems and solutions. Try to make sure that the solution you are offering matches a problem that your learners are likely to have. Offering solutions where there isn't a problem is the wrong way round, like the tail wagging the dog.

To put it another way: we need to be selective about what we present to our classes. We don't need to teach a pronunciation point simply because it exists, or because we've got a great piece of material on that topic. The point of pronunciation teaching is not to cover everything, but to cover what's needed.

The temptation to teach everything is at its strongest where there is a clear *set* of items – the **phonemic** alphabet being a good example. When the symbols are packaged into their cells in the chart like chocolates in a box, they all seem to have equivalent importance. That is not a helpful impression. Some phonemes do much more work than others, being more common or being more crucial in meaning distinctions – they have a higher '**functional load**'. This would suggest they should be awarded higher priority. Furthermore, how problematic a phoneme is will depend on the first language of the student, and this too should be taken into account. Some phonemes will need work; others are never likely to be problematic. There are some chocolates we can just leave in the box!

Some solutions are so neat that they tempt you to manufacture a problem to go with them. For example, there is a group of two-syllable words which are both nouns and verbs, where the stress falls on the first syllable for the noun and the second for the verb. These include words like *produce*, *rebel*, *export* and *record*. Students and teachers love a tidy rule like this, but if you find yourself teaching this vocabulary simply so that you can teach the rule, you know something is wrong: the 'tail is wagging the dog'.

There is also a temptation to launch into a full presentation of a pronunciation point the first time a problem emerges, when a reduced version might be more appropriate. For example, the pronunciation of past tense endings (*-ed*) may be expressed as a rule with two parts:

1   Pronounce *-ed* as an extra syllable if the root verb ends with /d/ or /t/ (e.g. *wanted*, *needed*).

2   For other verbs, pronounce *-ed* as /t/ if the root verb ends with an unvoiced consonant (e.g. *walked*, *laughed*) and otherwise /d/ (e.g. *loved*, *called*).

When your learners first start using past tense forms, it is probably appropriate to teach part 1 of the rule. Part 2 may be left for another time, perhaps when part 1 is being recycled later in the course. What I'm saying is that you can be selective, not only about *which* rules or patterns you present but also about *how much* of them you present at any one time.

In choosing what rules or parts of rules to present first, a useful concept is '**surrender value**'. What this amounts to is the following: imagine that your learners suddenly have to quit the course tomorrow. Which pronunciation points would be most indispensable to take away with them right now? I suggested that part 1 of the *-ed* rule should come first because the consequences of 'getting it wrong' are more serious in terms of intelligibility. Part 2 can be left for later because the consequences would be less serious, or because learners are simply less likely to 'get it wrong'.

Brown, A. (1991) *Functional Load* (pp. 211–224) in *Teaching English Pronunciation*. London: Routledge.

Don't be afraid to simplify

> **Just as with grammar, it is sometimes useful to give simple rules for pronunciation, even if the rules are not entirely accurate.**

'Murphy's Law' is the way people jokingly refer to the apparent law of nature that if something could possibly go wrong, it *will* go wrong. A version of this for the classroom could be: 'If you give the class a rule, the first thing the learners will find are the exceptions'. For example, if you give them this rule: 'We pronounce *sh* as /ʃ/', a bright learner will immediately find exceptions such as *dishonest* or *mishap*.

Teachers who have been embarrassed by exceptions may react in two ways – fight or flight. *Fight* is to restate the rule so that exceptions are excluded, for example, adding that 'the *s* and the *h* must be in the same morpheme'. *Flight* is to avoid giving the rule altogether. The problem with the first option is that the rule just gets too long and complicated to explain. The problem with the second is that we deprive our learners of an empowering insight which can speed up their learning.

In pronunciation, just as in grammar, a clear and simple rule is useful, even if it is not entirely accurate and has exceptions. It can provide a foothold on the learning curve, and it can always be refined later as the learner progresses. Pronunciation rules are of various kinds, and they are simplified in various different ways. Let's have a look at a few contrasting examples, along with exceptions and explanations.

1 A spelling rule

'The final *e* in words like *plane*, *site* and *rode* means that the vowel before is pronounced as it is in the alphabet (A = /eɪ/, I = /aɪ/, O = /əʊ/).'
   Exceptions: *have*, *give*, *gone* …

English spelling patterns have exceptions because in many cases the pronunciation has changed over time while spellings have remained as they were. Note that the exceptions in this instance happen to be very common words, so learners will come across them straight away. In this case, it may be best to give some exceptions at the same time as presenting the rule!

2   A word stress rule

'Ninety percent of two-syllable nouns have the stress on the first syllable.'
   Exceptions: *guitar, dessert, machine …*

English **word stress** often reflects the historical origins of words –
whether they come from German, French or Greek roots, for example.
In this instance, it may be best to present the rule with 'most' or 'ninety
percent' to show that there may be exceptions.

3   An articulation rule

'When you say the sounds /p/, /t/ and /k/, there is a puff of air from the
mouth – you can feel it if you put your hand in front of your mouth.'
   Exceptions: *spin, store, school …*

The puff of air with these consonants is known as **aspiration**, and it
only occurs at the beginning of a syllable – which is not the case in the
exceptions above. It is nevertheless a useful rule, especially in trying to
distinguish these consonants from /b/, /d/ and /g/.

4   Rhythm and stress rules

'Pronounce **content words** strongly and **function words** weakly.'
   Exceptions: *What are YOU doing here?* (contrasting 'you' with
   another person).

This rule expresses a normal, or 'default' situation. However, this rule
of rhythm can be overridden by another, higher-level rule relating to
contrastive stress, which creates the 'exception' above. I would present
these two rules separately as they can be confusing all at once.

5   An intonation rule

'The intonation usually goes down at the end of *Wh-* questions.'
   Exceptions: *Where did you say you're from?* (checking information
   you already have).

This is a rule of coincidence rather than cause. The 'cause' of intonation
is in the communicative context rather than the grammar (see Tip 29).
It just so happens that the context of *Wh-* questions often means that a
falling intonation is appropriate for them. This is a very weak kind of
rule, and yet I use it sometimes because it's a useful starting point.

Show how sounds are made

16

> At the heart of pronunciation teaching is showing learners
> how to make the sounds of the target language. The
> challenges are different for consonant sounds and for
> vowel sounds.

I always think that if sounds were a picture, **consonants** would be
the lines and **vowels** would be the colours. The lines create the shapes
and the colours fill in the spaces between. In this tip, I'll outline which
aspects of consonant and vowel sounds that we need to devote time to
in class, leaving the more practical presentation techniques to Tip 37.

Consonant sounds: place of articulation

To show learners how to make consonants, you will need to make them
aware of the key vocal organs: the lips, teeth, tongue and the roof of the
mouth, from the **alveolar ridge** at the front to the **soft palate** at the back.

Sounds involving the lips and teeth are relatively easy to demonstrate in
that they are visible. You can point to the lips being pressed together for the
sound /m/, or the top teeth pressed into the bottom lip for the sound /f/.

Sounds which are made further back inside the mouth like /s/ or /g/
are less easy to show because they're hidden from view. I'm probably
not the only pronunciation teacher to wish that we had windows in
our cheeks to make consonants easier to demonstrate! Without such
windows, we have to make do with cross-section diagrams showing
a head in profile, cut in half so that we can see inside the mouth – see
Appendix 3.

Consonant sounds: manner of articulation

A fundamental distinction can be made between consonants in which
the flow of air is stopped completely for a moment (the **stops**), and
those in which the air is allowed to squeeze through a narrow gap (the
fricatives). Demonstrate to learners how fricative sounds like /f/ can be
extended indefinitely, while stop sounds like /t/ cannot. A third category

of consonants involves the air being diverted out through the nose (the **nasals**, such as /m/).

Another important distinction is between the **voiced** and **unvoiced** consonant pairs, such as /b/ and /p/ or /z/ and /s/. In these pairs, the first sound involves making the vocal cords vibrate while the second doesn't.

A final feature which learners should be aware of is **aspiration**. This is the puff of air which comes out of the mouth with initial unvoiced stop consonants, especially /p/ and /t/. This is noticeable if you put your hand in front of your mouth as you say them.

Vowel sounds

Vowel sounds are harder to show than consonants because there are no exact points of contact in the mouth. The quality of these sounds depends on the size and shape of the mouth space, and this is controlled by three moving parts – the jaw, the lips and the tongue.

Jaw movement is fairly easy to demonstrate. For example, put your finger on your nose and your thumb on your chin. Then say /iː/ followed by /ɑː/. The finger and thumb will be forced apart as the jaw opens. Lip shape is also easy to show, for example by comparing the spread lips in /iː/ and the round lips in /uː/.

Tongue position, on the other hand, is difficult to show because it's invisible. Cross-section mouth diagrams may be useful for some learners, but others find them hard to interpret – many of us can't really imagine what our tongues are doing as we speak. However, see the suggestions in Tip 37.

Vowel sounds also differ in their manner of articulation. Some involve muscular tension and may be pronounced longer (the **tense**, or long vowels). Others can be pronounced with a more relaxed mouth and may be shorter (the **lax**, or short vowels).

Finally, learners need to be aware that some vowels are produced with the mouth in a fixed shape (the pure vowels), while others involve the mouth starting in one position and then moving to another position (the **diphthongs**).

Roach, P. (2000) *English Phonetics and Phonology: A practical guide, 4th edition.*
Cambridge: Cambridge University Press.

Show how phonemes change meaning

Phonemes are sounds which contribute to meaning differences. When presenting and practising them, it's best to do so in a context which makes this link with meaning clear. This is why minimal pairs are so useful in pronunciation teaching.

In one episode of the British TV comedy 'Blackadder', a character is attempting to write a dictionary. For the word *dog*, he provides the definition, 'not a cat'. As a definition, this is so ridiculous that the audience laughs. However, I think a defining style like this can actually be very useful in pronunciation because individual phonemes really need to be demonstrated *in contrast* to others. An essential part of understanding the pronunciation of *dog*, for example, is knowing that it is not *dock*. Similarly, *cat* is not *cut*.

The notion of *contrast* is present in the very idea of **phoneme**, unlike the similar term *sound*. Let me explain: in an American **accent**, the *t* in *town* is pronounced as the sound [t], while in *city* it is usually pronounced [ɾ] (the square brackets show that these are sounds). The two sounds don't contrast: they are both variants of the phoneme /t/ (the slash brackets show that this is a phoneme). There is a contrast, however, between the /t/ in *town* and the /d/ in *down* – the two phonemes correspond to a difference in meaning. (Note: two sounds which are contrasting phonemes in one language may not be in another.)

Pairs of words which differ only in one phoneme like *down* and *town* or *dog* and *dock* are known as **minimal pairs**, and they are very useful in pronunciation teaching because they clearly demonstrate to learners how pronunciation can have an impact on meaning. For example, if you say, *The dogs are dangerous*, but don't distinguish the phonemes /g/ and /k/, the listener may think you are talking about the docks being dangerous.

Sceptics suggest that in reality, minimal pairs are not important because people can usually guess the meaning from context. For example, if someone says, *Do you prefer docks or cats?* you probably know what they mean. It is certainly true that listeners can tolerate a few merged phonemes. For example, many Londoners don't distinguish *three* from *free*, and yet they remain intelligible. Similarly, many Scots pronounce *pull* like *pool*, and many speakers in the US merge *cot* and *caught*.

The problem is that every time two phonemes are merged into one, the balance tips a little bit more in the direction of misunderstanding. With every lost pixel, the picture gets less clear. You can get away with one or two lost phonemes, but learners often have more issues than that. Unintelligible speech is usually the result of a tangle of different pronunciation problems, but teachers can only tackle them one by one.

Although the safest bet is to help learners to distinguish as many phonemes as possible, some distinctions are more important than others. Indeed, some can probably be ignored for most purposes. An example of this is the distinction between the **vowel** phonemes /ʊə/ in *poor* and /ɔː/ in *pour*. Only a minority of speakers of English still make this distinction, the majority preferring to use /ɔː/ for both. For this reason, I don't include /ʊə/ in my version of the phonemic chart (see Appendix 2).

To sum up: I think we need to present phonemes as a set of meaningful contrasts. Here are some practical suggestions of how to go about that:

- Present pairs or groups of phonemes so that learners notice how they contrast with each other.
- Illustrate how phonemes affect meaning by choosing pairs of words or phrases which differ in just one single sound (minimal pairs).
- Show how phonemes relate to others in the system as a whole by using a chart (see Tip 22).
- Use practice activities in which the outcome depends on accurately distinguishing phonemes, receptively and productively (see Tip 40).
- In feedback to learners, don't say 'correct' or 'incorrect'; say 'that works' or 'that could be misunderstood' (see Tip 33).

Understand that sounds vary in context

18

> You should be aware of some of the ways in which sounds
> are affected by neighbouring sounds in words. Learners
> will need to master some of these productively. For others,
> a receptive awareness is sufficient.

Let me brighten your day with my first three examples: *sunlight*,
sunbathe and *sunglasses*. Notice that the first syllable in the first
example sounds like *sun*, but in the second and third examples it may
sound like *sum* and *sung*. Why is that? It seems like a clear case of a
sound (in this case, the **consonant** *n*) being influenced by its neighbours
(in this case, the following consonant).

Sometimes, when two sounds occur in sequence, they tend to blend
together to become one. For example, the sequence *tu* in words like
future, *culture* or *situation* would once have been pronounced with the
consonant cluster of /t/ followed by /j/. For most speakers nowadays, the
two consonants have merged together into the single phoneme /tʃ/.

A sound may also be influenced by its position in the syllable. For example,
the /l/ normally sounds different at the beginning and ending of a word –
compare *lip* and *pill*. The latter is called the *dark l*, and is sometimes lost
altogether, turning into a vowel so the word sounds like 'piw'.

Although the examples above are interesting, learners probably don't
need to master these variations productively. However, some contextual
variations *are* important for learners to master, and here are three
examples.

Past tense endings

Although there is a **vowel** in the spelling, the -*ed* ending is normally
pronounced simply as a /d/ or a /t/. The choice is determined by the
neighbouring sounds: if the verb ends with an **unvoiced** consonant, the
-*ed* is pronounced /t/ as in *walked*. Otherwise, the -*ed* is pronounced
/d/ as in *played*. However, there is a third option where the vowel *is*

pronounced: when the verb ends with /t/ or /d/, the -ed is pronounced /ɪd/ as in *wanted* or *needed*. This option is interesting – it seems that if two consonants are too similar to each other, they don't like to be neighbours (more on this in Tip 30).

Vowel clipping before unvoiced consonants

Unvoiced consonants, especially /p/, /t/ and /k/, have the effect of shortening the vowel before them, so that *pup*, *mat* and *lock* sound more clipped than *pub*, *mad* and *log*. Some learners find it useful to deliberately clip the vowels in this way, because it can be very difficult to distinguish **voiced** and unvoiced consonants at the end of a word otherwise. However, if your learners have no problem distinguishing final consonants, you probably don't need to mention the vowel shortening. In pronunciation teaching, it is often wisest to work on a 'need-to-know' basis – you don't need to teach what learners don't need to know.

Aspiration

Another important variation which affects how sounds are realised is **aspiration**. When the consonants /p/, /t/ and /k/ occur at the beginning of a stressed syllable, they are pronounced with a puff of air which is strong enough to feel if put your hand in front of your mouth. However, that puff of air is absent when the same phonemes occur in a consonant cluster after *s*, for example *sport*, *stand* or *scream*. Nor does it occur at the end of a word. Thus, if you want to mention aspiration as a way to help learners produce a difference between phoneme pairs like /p/ and /b/, /t/ and /d/ or /k/ and /g/, make sure the examples you choose have those sounds at the beginning of the word!

I mentioned above that there are some features of contextual variation that learners don't need to master *productively*. However, awareness of them could be very useful *receptively* (for their listening skills). We will look more closely at these kinds of variations in Tip 26 on connected speech.

Be aware of accent variation

> English is an international language with a great deal of
> accent variation. Teachers need to be aware of some of the
> ways that pronunciation varies across different accents
> in order to help learners become flexible users of the
> language.

English is such a widely spoken language in the world today that **accent**
variation is to be expected, and we need to work with this variation, not
against it. Just as an earthquake resistant building is built to withstand
movement, we need our approach to pronunciation teaching to be
flexible and accent-tolerant. Teachers need to find out about the ways in
which accents often vary.

In this tip, rather than attempting to look at any specific accent in detail,
we will look at some specific **phonemes** which have a strong tendency
to vary across many different accents of English. I won't distinguish
between 'native speaker' and 'non-native speaker' accents, since learners
will need to be tolerant of both equally.

1   /r/: This phoneme is perhaps the one which is most variable across
    English accents. In some accents, such as American English, the
    tongue tip is curled back. In others such as in Scottish or Spanish
    English, the tongue tip flicks against the **alveolar ridge**. Yet other
    accents such as French English create a /r/ with the back of the
    tongue rather than the tip. English and Australian English drops the
    /r/ altogether when there is no **vowel** sound to follow it.
2   /t/: This phoneme is very vulnerable to variation in some positions.
    For example, between vowels in American, it may change to
    something like a /d/, so that *waiting* sounds like *wading*. In the UK,
    it is often replaced by a **glottal stop** – a brief silence caused by a
    closing of the throat, so that *Britain* sounds like *Bri'n*.
3   /θ/ and /ð/: These sounds are avoided in many accents. They are
    often replaced by /f/ and /v/ in London, by /t/ and /d/ in Ireland or
    by /s/ and /z/ in France and Germany.

4 /h/: This is often dropped in Welsh and Italian accents, so that *hill* sounds like *ill*. However, in Welsh and Scottish there *is* a /h/ sound at the beginning of words which begin with *wh* such as *where* and *why*.

5 /j/: This disappears in some contexts in North America, so that *tune* sounds like *toon*. In British English, this word begins with the **consonant cluster** /tj/ or the phoneme /ʧ/.

6 /ɒ/: The vowel sound in *hot, shop* or *long* is short, made with rounded lips in England, but long with wide lips in North America – it is one of the most noticeable differences between these two accents. In American, it would be better represented by the symbol /ɑ/.

7 /æ/: The vowel sound in *bag, mad* or *cat* is produced with the jaw less open in Australia and New Zealand so that *bag* sounds like *beg*. In the UK, it is a short vowel, while in the US it is longer and may bend like a **diphthong**.

8 /ʌ/: For this phoneme, as you move south to north through England, the jaw opens less. In the south, it is very wide so that *luck* sounds like *lack*. In the north it is much less open so that *luck* sounds like *look*.

9 /eɪ/ and /əʊ/: These diphthongs are characterised by a bend caused by the mouth changing position. But in some accents, they don't bend, so that for example *stay* sounds like **RP** *stair* and *coat* sounds like RP *caught*. This happens in Scotland and the north of England.

10 /ɑː/: In RP, this vowel is found in a set of words including *grass, castle* or *fast*. In many other accents, these words have the same vowel sound as *bag, mad* or *cat*. This is a noticeable difference between the south and north of England, for example.

Wells, J. C. (1982) *Accents of English 1: An Introduction.* Cambridge: Cambridge University Press.

Decide whether to use phonemic symbols

20

> Using phonemic symbols can be very useful in pronunciation work, but it isn't obligatory. There are points in favour and points against, and in the end, your decision will depend on your context.

Exotic-looking **phonemic symbols** are almost an icon of pronunciation, but that shouldn't blind us to the fact that we have choice: it's perfectly possible to teach pronunciation without them. Accordingly, in this tip we will take the symbols to court and examine the case for and against using them with learners.

For

- In some languages, spelling is a reliable guide to pronunciation. However, in English, it is not. Phonemic symbols offer us a less ambiguous way to represent sounds.
- Learners can see the complete set of symbols for English, and this helps to make the learning task more finite. Otherwise, there might appear to be an almost never-ending set of possible sounds in the language.
- Many of us trust our eyes more than our ears. For example, learners may be convinced that they hear the *e* in *walked* no matter how many times they hear the word. However, when they see the phonemic spelling /wɔːkt/, it's instantly clear and 'official'.
- Familiarity with symbols can increase learner autonomy. IPA symbols, for example, are widely used in dictionaries and other published materials.
- Once learners have started to become familiar with the symbols, teachers' explanations can become much faster and more efficient.
- In the absence of phonemic symbols, learners are more tempted to represent pronunciation using their own personal spellings. These spellings do not always distinguish between two similar sounds. For example, a learner might represent both *feel* and *fill* as *fil*. A quick fix like this can lead to a problem in the longer term.

- The odd appearance of the symbols may serve to highlight to learners that we are focusing on sound, not orthography.

Against

- Learners already have enough to learn, without loading them down with a set of strange symbols (especially if the Roman alphabet is also new to them, as it might be, for example, for Arabic and Chinese learners).
- Using symbols is quite daunting and analytical. Sometimes a more intuitive approach may be more suitable, especially with young learners.
- There are alternatives. For example, we could use 'key words' instead of symbols to represent a phoneme (see the key words in my chart in Appendix 2).
- Time spent learning symbols can be wasted if you can't guarantee continuity. For example, if a class has many different teachers and only one of them uses the symbols, the benefit is reduced.
- Learning the full set of symbols is a long-term investment. Some learning encounters are only short term – for example, a learner going to the UK for a couple of weeks at a language school.
- In some classes, some of the learners are familiar with the symbols while others have never seen them before. It is hard to make consistent use of symbols in this circumstance.

The Verdict

It depends on context. I'm sure nobody will be surprised by this conclusion, but it's clear from the points above that a 'one-size-fits-all' approach won't work here. You need to consider learners' age, language background and previous learning experience. You also need to bear in mind how long you are going to be with your group of learners, and whether the symbols are used consistently across your school.

However, a final point I would make in summing up this case is that use of symbols doesn't have to be all-or-nothing. In my current teaching situation, for example, I often have to work with short-stay learners. I usually deal with symbols lightly, using the symbols in a way which doesn't assume previous familiarity with them on the part of the learners, and avoiding activities which are solely focused on teaching symbols.

Be clear about what phonemic symbols represent

21

> Phonemic symbols do not represent precise sounds, but rather a range of sounds which are considered to be the same in a language. It is unhelpful for pronunciation teachers to treat the symbols as if they are exact.

Phonemic symbols can be very useful in pronunciation teaching, but they can also be very misleading. Teachers often believe that the symbols represent very specific sounds. In fact a symbol represents an area rather than a precise point. Consider this analogy: if somebody asks you where France is, it is not very helpful to give them GPS coordinates. France is not a single point but an area. It might be more useful to say that it is a country in Western Europe.

This misunderstanding about the nature of phonemic symbols has two unfortunate consequences for language teaching:

1 It can put teachers off the symbols, and pronunciation teaching generally.
2 It can encourage a prescriptive approach to accent.

Let's look at each of these in turn.

1 At the start of my teaching career, I was introduced to the International Phonetic Association (IPA) symbols which are often used in coursebooks published in Britain. I found some of the symbols very puzzling. For example, the /ʌ/ symbol which represents the **vowel** sound in *cut*: when I tried to make that sound, I found it did not match the *cut* vowel of Received Pronunciation (**RP**) – the British standard. This left me with a doubt which could easily have put me off pronunciation teaching: would I have to change my **accent** in order to teach this stuff? Now I think it is much more useful to take a flexible view: the /ʌ/ symbol represents the vowel sound in *cut*, whatever the accent. In other words, it represents a range of vowel sounds.

2   If we take the symbols to represent precise sounds, then they will only be able to represent one accent. This can lead to some very prescriptive classroom activities, with the teacher directing the learners' attention to the exact quality of the sounds. It is much more useful to be flexible about the sound's quality and focus instead on how it compares and contrasts with the other **phonemes** in the chart.

A phoneme is like a chess piece. The knight, for example, can be many different shapes in different chess sets, but that doesn't affect how the piece functions – what is important is how the piece moves in the game.

It is tempting to be over-precise about interpreting symbols whichever system you choose, but perhaps most especially with IPA symbols mentioned above. It may be useful to go into a little more detail to understand the reason for this.

The IPA **phonetic symbols** were created to represent *all* possible sounds in all languages. They are specific enough to describe differences between phonemes in different accents of the same language too. For most language teaching purposes, the complete set of phonetic symbols is unnecessary. Instead, we use *phonemic* symbols – these only show the meaningful sounds in *one* language – the **target language**. Phonemic symbols may be identical to phonetic symbols, but they appear between slash brackets, e.g. /e/, while phonetic symbols appear between square brackets, [e]. The temptation to be over-precise happens when we confuse the two and treat phonemic symbols as if they were phonetic.

The important thing for us teachers is to use the symbols flexibly and not waste time with irrelevant detail. To return to the example of the /ʌ/ symbol: we shouldn't be too concerned about its exact phonetic quality. Instead, we should focus on the fact that it represents the vowel sound in *cut* as opposed to the vowel sounds in similar words such as *caught* or *coot*. If a learner can pronounce the phoneme sufficiently clearly to make those distinctions, that should be enough – even if their pronunciation doesn't sound exactly like the model.

A phonemic chart is more than just a list of symbols, it is also very effective in showing how the phonemes relate to one another. It's worth spending a little time getting to know how the chart is organised.

If you are going to use a chart, find out how it is organised and, where appropriate, explain it to learners. In this tip, I will describe the basic organising principles of a typical chart, and the reasons why I think it is beneficial for teaching and learning.

Vowels

The **vowel** diagram which is the prototype for many modern **phonemic** charts was developed by linguist Daniel Jones, but many teachers will be more familiar with the classroom-friendly version by Adrian Underhill (Appendix 1). It is a squared shape representing the space inside a mouth in profile, facing towards the left. The vowel symbols are placed in the square. If the symbol is:

- on the left side of the square, it is made with the mouth wide and tongue forward.
- on the right side of the square, it is made with the mouth rounded and tongue back.
- near the top of the square, it is made with the jaw more closed and tongue up.
- near the bottom of the square, it is made with the jaw wide open and tongue down.
- in the middle of the square, it is made with the mouth in a neutral position.

My own version of the vowel chart (Appendix 2) has a hexagonal structure, but the same organisational principles hold.

Consonants

Consonant symbols are often presented in pairs, with the **voiced** and **unvoiced** sounds in adjacent boxes. These pairs may be ordered according to the place in the mouth where the sound is articulated. For example, in the Underhill chart the consonants, like the vowels, are organised so that on the left of the chart are the sounds made towards the front of the mouth (consonants like /p/ and /b/) while to the right are the sounds made towards the back of the mouth (consonants like /k/ and /g/). The **stop** consonants are on one row and the **fricatives** on the next.

Benefits

The main benefits of using a phonemic chart with your learners are, I think, as follows:

1 **Memory.** Many of us remember frequently-used phone or pin numbers not just from the numbers themselves, but also from their position on the keypad. Similarly, as learners begin to get familiar with the chart, many will remember the phonemes not just from the shape of the symbols but also from their position. Symbol and position reinforce each other in the memory.

2 **Orientation.** Compare a map with a map's index (a list of all the places on the map in alphabetical order). Both documents have all the same names written on them, but the map has much more information; it shows not only the places but also the spatial relationships *between* them. Similarly, a well-designed chart shows much more than just a list of phonemes – it also shows how they relate to one another, giving the learner a sense of the sound system as a whole.

3 **Exploration.** You can use the chart as a basis for exploring the sound system. For example, point at one phoneme and ask learners to make that sound. Then move your finger from that phoneme to a neighbouring one. Ask learners to make those two sounds one after the other and focus their attention on what changes they must make in their mouth to achieve this change. The fact that two phonemes are next to each other on the chart usually means that they are similar in some ways but different in at least one, and this kind of activity draws attention to the difference.

4 **Appeal.** For most people, a graphic such as a chart is much more eye-catching than a simple list. A phonemic chart can provoke curiosity; a plain set of phonemic symbols is much less likely to do so. A chart is much more worthy of a place on your classroom wall than just a list!

Underhill, A. (2005) *Sound Foundations*. Oxford: Macmillan.

English spelling can appear confusing for learners – sometimes it matches the pronunciation, and sometimes not. However, there are some spelling patterns which can be very useful to know.

English pronunciation has changed over time, while spelling has remained relatively fixed. As a result, there is no simple correspondence between spelling and sound, and this can be very frustrating for learners. However, there *are* useful patterns which you can point out to learners.

Short vowels and alphabet vowels: When you say the letters of the alphabet, the **vowel** letters are pronounced like this:

A = /eɪ/, E = /iː/, I = /aɪ/, O = /əʊ/, U = /juː/. We could call these five vowel sounds the 'alphabet vowels'. However, in one-syllable words with a **consonant** at the end, they are usually pronounced as short vowel sounds:

A = /æ/ e.g. *tap*, E = /e/ e.g. *pet*, I = /ɪ/ e.g. *win*, O = /ɒ/ e.g. *hop*, U = /ʌ/ e.g. *cut*.

The 'magic *e*' rule: A useful spelling pattern is this: when you add an *e* to the end of words like the examples above, the pronunciation changes from short vowel to an alphabet vowel, for example *tap – tape, pet – Pete, win – wine, hop – hope, cut – cute*. But be warned: the main exceptions to this rule happen to be some very common words, e.g. *have, live, come, gone*. If you don't tell learners about these exceptions, it won't be long before they find them for themselves!

Vowel digraphs: Two vowel letters together are called *vowel digraphs*. Sometimes the pronunciation can be predicted because they are the alphabet pronunciation of the first of the two letters:

ai = /eɪ/ e.g. *plain*, *ea* = /iː/ e.g. *heat*, *ie* = /aɪ/ e.g. *lie*, *oa* = /əʊ/ e.g. *coat*, *ui* = /uː/ e.g. *fruit*. But be warned: all of these vowel digraphs have other possible pronunciations too. Some digraphs have many possible pronunciations – perhaps the most notorious is the digraph *ou*, which is pronounced differently in all six of these words: *soul, house, trouble, soup, cough, fought.*

Homophones: Obviously, if the alphabet vowel sounds can be spelt with either the 'magic *e*' or a vowel digraph, then we may get **homophones** – pairs of words with the same pronunciation but different spelling such as *plane* and *plain*. I find that learners are sometimes quite shocked to discover that homophones are possible. However, they usefully illustrate the point that English spelling does not match pronunciation.

R-vowels: When a letter *r* comes after a vowel, it is pronounced in some accents and not in others. But either way, it changes the sound of the vowel before it. For example, the following words all have short or alphabet vowel sound: *cat, pea, bee, pot, hut*. However, if you add an *r* after the vowel, the sound changes: *cart* /ɑ:/, *pear* /eə/, *beer* /ɪə/, *port* /ɔ:/, *hurt* /ɜ:/. I call these five sounds the 'R-vowels'.

Doubled consonant rule: Doubled consonants often serve to show that the vowel before them is pronounced short. Compare these three words: *hid, hide, hidden*. The word *hid* has the short vowel /ɪ/, but *hide* has the alphabet vowel /aɪ/ following the 'magic *e*' rule. However, in *hidden*, the vowel is short again because of the doubled consonant rule.

Consonants: Letter *c*: is pronounced /k/ e.g. *cat*, but /s/ before *e, i* or *y*, e.g. *cinema*.

Letter *g*: is pronounced as /g/ e.g. *goat*, but as /dʒ/ before *e, i* or *y*, e.g. *gym*. Note that the *u* in words like *guest* is silent but it prevents the *g* from becoming /dʒ/.

Letter *s*: is /s/ at the start of a syllable e.g. *sun*, but /z/ at the end, e.g. *rise*.

Letter *h*: is often combined with another consonant letter to represent a sound, for example *ch* in *chip*, *ph* in *phone*, *sh* in *shop*, *th* in *thing*. It is sometimes silent e.g. *hour*.

Letters *y* and *w*: these are consonant sounds at the start of a syllable e.g. *yes*, *watch*, but vowel sounds at the end, e.g. *pay*, *how*. *W* is sometimes silent e.g. *write*.

Silent letters: these include *b*, e.g. *climb*, *k*, e.g. *knife*, *l*, e.g. *half*, *n*, e.g. *autumn*, *p*, e.g. *receipt*, *s*, e.g. *island*, *t*, e.g. *listen*.

Carney, E. (1997) *English Spelling*. London: Routledge.

Focus on word stress

> If a word has more than one syllable, one of them is normally stronger than the others. This is known as *word stress*. Although the rules of word stress in English are complex, there are some patterns which may help learners.

In words with more than one syllable, some syllables are weak and others are strong. Like the mountains in a landscape, the strong syllables stand prominent. Many learners will notice this prominence intuitively, but others may need help. If their own language does not differentiate weak and strong syllables, learners may be 'stress deaf'. You will need to raise their awareness of how strong syllables are louder, longer and higher in **pitch**.

Many of the underlying patterns of **word stress** are too complex to be useful but there are some which are worth focusing on, and we will look at these here.

Two-syllable nouns: These tend to have stress at the beginning, for example *lemon*. I often use circles to represent syllables, with a big circle for the stressed syllable – so *lemon* would be **Oo**.

Two-syllable verbs: These tend to have stress at the end, for example *forget* – **oO**. However, there are plenty of exceptions such as *listen* or *answer*. Exceptions can sometimes be explained because syllables such as *-en* or *-er* are inherently weak. But it may be best to let learners pick up this insight through experience rather than by explicit teaching.

Noun-verb pairs: Some words like *insult* and *record* may be both nouns (with the pattern **Oo**) and verbs (with the pattern **oO**). If these are worth teaching at all, it is not because they are important in themselves (this is not a very big group of words) but because they illustrate so clearly the general pattern for two-syllable nouns and verbs.

Stress-neutral suffixes: Think of a set of related words like *forget*, *forgetful*, *forgetfulness*, *unforgettable*. If you know the stress pattern of the root word – the two-syllable verb *forget* – you also know where to place the stress in the longer words. I think it is useful for students to be made aware of this.

Stress-changing suffixes: Look at this set of related words: *nation, nationality, nationalise, nationalisation, nationalist, nationalistic*. The stress is on the beginning of the two-syllable noun *nation*, but on some of the longer words, it moves because some of the suffixes change the stress. The stress moves to the syllable immediately before the suffixes *-ion*, *-ic* and *-ity*. This is a teachable pattern.

Stress in compound nouns: In compound nouns, the stress is usually on the stressed syllable of the first element, for example, *traffic light* and *newspaper* both have the pattern **Ooo**. This is also true for nouns with two distinct elements like *photograph*. But note that word combinations like *plastic bag* and *kitchen sink*, where the first gives the material or location of the second, have a stressed syllable in both words.

Shifting stress: I think that we as teachers should be aware that the stress of a word in context does not always match the stress of that word as cited in a dictionary. For example, *seventeen* has the pattern **ooO** and *years* has the pattern **O**. When you put them together, you would expect the pattern to be **ooOO**. However, in this context, you can't really hear a stress on *-teen*, so it sounds like **oooO** and it may sound like **OoooO**. If you are going to teach the stress pattern of words like *seventeen* (and I think we should), just be careful in choosing the contexts you use to present and practise it!

Optional stress: Some words which are stressed at the end in British English are stressed at the beginning in American English, for example *magazine* and *cigarette*. There is an increasing tendency for British speakers to follow the American pattern for such words. Where stress patterns vary across accents or even within the same **accent** like this, I would leave it as optional for the learners – it doesn't matter which way they go.

Many accents of English have a characteristic rhythm because some words are pronounced strongly and others weakly. It is useful for learners to be aware of this, not necessarily for their own speech, but certainly for listening purposes.

English can be divided into **content words** and **function words**. Content words include items such as nouns, adjectives and main verbs. Function words (sometimes called 'grammar words') include items such as prepositions, pronouns, the verb *to be* and auxiliary verbs. In many native **accents** of English, including the 'standard' accents, the content words tend to be strongly pronounced while the function words tend to be pronounced weakly, and this gives the language a characteristic rhythm.

If your students are planning to live or spend time in an English speaking country, then learning to speak with this rhythm will probably make them more comfortably intelligible to the locals. But even if they have no such plans, becoming familiar with rhythm will help them to understand speakers from those countries more effectively.

The rhythm of English is not usually regular enough to be very noticeable in natural speech, but it is often exaggerated in rhymes, poems and chants, making these very useful for teaching purposes. Teachers of young learners often use nursery rhymes, while other kinds of rhymes such as limericks may be suitable for older age groups.

When using rhymes, be aware that the rhythm is not always natural. For example, limericks often begin with a line such as *There **was** a young woman from **Wales**.* The function word *was* is pronounced strongly here, which is not ideal.

While rhymes, poems and chants are useful for highlighting rhythm, they don't generally include the kinds of phrases that students are going to find useful in everyday exchanges such as engaging in small talk with a colleague or ordering a meal. However, there are rhymes specifically written for teaching which include this kind of language, such as Carolyn Graham's *Jazz Chants* (see below).

Rhymes and chants are useful, and in my experience, learners usually find them enjoyable too. However, they are not to everybody's taste, and there are other ways of helping learners to notice rhythm. I often use a technique which I call 'micro-drilling'. This involves either playing back a very short extract from an audio, over and over, or simply repeating a short phrase myself for the students to repeat. The multiple repetition serves to highlight the natural rhythm in the phrase. Let's say, for example, that the phrase is **Where do you live?** If you repeat this four, five, six times, then a rhythm emerges like the sound of a train going along a track: OooO, OooO, OooO, OooO. This reflects the rule that the content words *where* and *live* are strong while the function words *do* and *you* are weak. This train rhythm is very common in simple *Wh-* questions and I think of it as a kind of audible grammar.

You can also take a more explicit approach to teaching rhythm. Present the content / function word rule to the students. In *PronPack* (see below), I use the metaphor of bricks and cement: the content words are strong and keep their shape, like bricks, while the function words are weak and get crushed between, like the cement. From the listener's perspective, it is the function words which are most difficult to catch because they get squashed out of shape and hard to recognise. It is worth focusing attention on how these function words are distorted (there's more detail on this in Tip 26). For example, say the numbers 1–4 with very common sequences of function words in between and get the learners to repeat. For example:

ONE for a TWO for a THREE for a FOUR

ONE was in TWO was in THREE was in FOUR

ONE has been TWO has been THREE has been FOUR

Here, the content words are replaced by a very predictable sequence of numbers, meaning that the learners' attention is free to focus on the sound of the function words.

Graham, C. (1978) *Jazz Chants*. New York: Oxford University Press.

Hancock, M. (2017) *PronPack 1: Pronunciation Workouts*. Chester: Hancock McDonald ELT.

Raise awareness of connected speech

26

> Words in connected speech sound different from words on their own. Learners need to be aware of the ways they sound in a joined-up context in order to improve their listening skills.

I think we imagine connected speech as words joined in sequence like a string of sausages, each sausage being one word. It's not like that. The words in connected speech are not so clearly distinguishable one from the next. Consider the following phrase: *Carrot sump at eight owes.* It looks like a string of five words, but in fact it's just an alternative way of 'hearing' the phrase, *carrots and potatoes.* Three words. The same continuous stream of sound can be interpreted either way.

Here are two more phrases which can sound identical:

A. *cooks and meals*
B. *cook some meals*

By analysing how these two phrases can possibly end up sounding the same, we can identify four key features of connected speech in English.

1 Linking

There's no difference between the pronunciation of *cooks and* and *cook sand.* That's because the /s/ in the phrase could equally well belong to *cook* or *and.* This is an example of **linking,** and it's especially noticeable in cases where one word ends with a **consonant** sound and the next word begins with a **vowel** sound.

2 Elision

There is a *d* in phrase A but not in B. This reflects the fact that in connected speech, the *d* in the word *and* is very often cut. This is sometimes reflected in informal spellings like *fish 'n' chips.* It's known as **elision.**

3 Assimilation

There is an /n/ in phrase A, but it becomes a /m/ in B. How is that possible? The answer lies in the next word *meals*, which begins with a /m/. The /d/ of *and* is cut, as we saw above. Then the /n/ changes to /m/ so that the lips are already together in preparation for the /m/ at the beginning of the next word. This is an example of what's known as **assimilation**.

4 Weak forms

The middle words in phrases A and B are both short **function words**, and these tend to be reduced to **weak forms** in connected speech. The most characteristic feature of a weak form is that the vowel tends to lose its distinctiveness and become /ə/, which is known as *schwa*. As a consequence, there is no difference between the vowel sound in *and* and *some* in connected speech. The other main feature of weak forms is elision, as we have already seen with the *d* in *and*. A consequence of reduced vowels plus elision means that the following four words – *a*, *her*, *or*, *of* – may all sound identical!

I called this tip *Raise awareness of connected speech* because I think this is especially important for listening. I would say these features are optional as regards your learners' own production – after all, in terms of intelligibility, speakers do not gain anything by cutting the *d* in *and*. On the contrary, it is probably clearer if they pronounce it.

However, if your learners use these features of connected speech in their own production, it might enable them to speak faster and perhaps sound more fluent. If these things are important to them, then they might want to adopt features of connected speech; it's their choice.

One way of raising awareness of these features is to show learners pairs of phrases which sound identical such as A and B above (I call these 'phrasal **homophones**'). Then explain or elicit the four key features listed above, just as I have done in this tip.

Be clear about sentence stress

27

> The term *sentence stress* is used ambiguously, which
> sometimes leads to confusion. We need to be clear about
> what it is and about how we present it.

I think there's often a lack of clarity about what sentence stress actually
is. There is a muddle because the term gets used in two different
contexts – rhythm, and intonation.

Rhythm: In Tip 25, we saw how English has a rhythm which is
characterised by **content words** being pronounced strongly and **function
words** pronounced weakly. Rhythm, like **word stress**, can be represented
by a pattern of big and small circles. So, for example, *I was working*
can be represented by the pattern ooOo. (The stressed syllable of the
content word *working* is a big circle; the function words *I* and *was*,
and the unstressed syllable *-ing* are small circles.) This rhythmic pattern
reflects the grammar of the phrase.

Intonation: One aspect of intonation is the placement of *tonic stress* in
the phrase (I'm using this term rather than the more ambiguous *sentence
stress*). Tonic stress is the special emphasis which a speaker puts on one
word in a phrase. There is usually just one syllable with tonic stress,
and the speaker can choose to place it anywhere. So, for example, if
somebody says, *You weren't working!*, you might reply, *I was working!*,
with stress on the positive *was* to contrast with the negative *weren't*.
In this example, you are using stress to focus the listener's attention on
the key word. I think it's better to avoid using patterns of big and small
circles to represent tonic stress so as not to confuse it with rhythm. Tonic
stress, unlike rhythm, is variable because it reflects the speaker's choice,

Rhythm and tonic stress: The tonic stress pattern of a phrase usually
reinforces the shape of the rhythm pattern. For example, the most likely
position of the tonic stress in *I was working* is on *working*, and this fits
nicely around the rhythmic shape ooOo. However, it's also possible to place
the tonic stress elsewhere in the phrase – for example, on the *was* in *I was
working*, and this means you can no longer hear the rhythmic shape of the

phrase. This is similar to the way that word stress patterns can be no longer audible in some contexts (see Tip 24). To sum up, tonic stress and rhythm are independent variables. Putting stress on a function word like *was* is done for a specific communicative effect known as ***contrastive stress***.

Contrastive stress: In the example sentences below, the tonic stress in A is neutral. It follows the 'rule' that tonic stress normally goes on the last content word of the phrase. That's because that's where the new information in the phrase is normally located, and the tonic stress is highlighting the new. Meanwhile, sentences B and C have contrastive stress, that is, they both break the rule in order to highlight a contrast.

A. *I was <u>working</u>.* (Answer to: *What were you doing?*)
B. *I <u>was</u> working!* (Response to: *You weren't working.*)
C. *<u>I</u> was working.* (Response to: *Nobody was working.*)

Teachers sometimes present contrastive stress, but fail to present the 'rule' – where to put the stress if you *don't* want to make a contrast. Learners can't always get it right by default – the rules in their **L1** may be quite different. Some languages like Korean don't make meaningful use of tonic stress at all. Others put it in a different place. Brazilian learners for example often put the tonic stress on the last word, even if it is not a content word. This can be a problem because it creates unintended contrastive stress. If you say, *I like <u>it</u>* (with stress on the *it*), the listener may think it's contrastive: *it* as opposed to what?

Explaining it simply: Learners find tonic stress hard. I think simplification is justified, even if it means creating non-authentic illustrative sentences. For example, the three sentences A–C above are identical in wording, which means that the learner's attention is focused on the only difference between them – the stress. On the other hand, they don't sound especially authentic. A more likely version of B for example might be, *I <u>was</u>, actually!* But that would complicate matters by bringing in another variable – the wording. Similarly, practice exercises may need to be a little inauthentic. For example, you could say sentences about a picture which are deliberately wrong and ask learners to correct you:

A: *The cat's on the table.*
B: *No, the cat's <u>under</u> the table!*

If you decide to work on intonation, you can take an approach which is intuitive, or one which is more analytical. Here, I will outline the first and then give more suggestions about the second.

In *The Importance of being Earnest*, a play by Irish author Oscar Wilde, a man confesses to his snobbish future mother-in-law that he never knew his parents and, as a baby, he was found at a railway station in a handbag. The woman is shocked and replies, 'A handbag?' If you were explaining to an actor how to deliver this line, you could suggest either of the following:

1 Say it with an incredulous tone of voice, as if checking you heard it right.
2 When you say the word *handbag*, start on a low **pitch** and then rise to a high pitch.

1 The intuitive approach

The first approach above is likely to work well with an actor. An actor, through intuition or training, knows how to express moods and attitudes through intonation. A non-actor might have more difficulty, especially if unfamiliar with the language and culture of the character in the play. A tone of voice which sounds 'incredulous' in one language might not sound that way in another.

Some language teachers take this intuitive approach to intonation, telling learners for example to 'say it in a polite tone of voice' or 'in a surprised voice'. Expressing mood in this way is sometimes known as the *attitudinal function* of intonation. This kind of activity may work perfectly well, and it's always worth trying. However, if the learner doesn't know intuitively what a polite tone of voice is (in English), there isn't much that the teacher can do to help, except demonstrate and hope the learner is a good mimic.

2   The analytical approach

The second approach benefits from not depending on intuition and cultural assumptions, making it potentially useful in a language teaching context. The analytical approach might however require a certain amount of training. People are not usually consciously aware of pitch movement in their speech, and it can take a lot of effort and attention to notice it, let alone control it. If you take an analytical approach, here are some basic suggestions:

a. Give learners the opportunity to play with **tone**. For example, get them to try saying a single word such as *really* with rising or falling tones, so they can get familiar with how these tones sound and feel.

b. Make a clear connection between tone and **tonic stress** (see Tip 27). The tone of a phrase remains almost level until you reach the tonic syllable. The rising or falling tone begins there.

c. Be clear about what the tone movement is. For example, in the phrase *I was found in a handbag*, the pitch of the voice will probably be level until it reaches *hand* and then jump up. The tone begins here and falls to the end of the sentence. However, learners may hear the jump up to *hand* and think that it's a rising tone. A line diagram on the board can help to clarify this.

d. Be aware of the fall-rise. The fall-rise is distinct from the rise, although I don't usually distinguish them for teaching purposes. However, learners sometimes fail to notice the rise at the end of the fall-rise – it can be very subtle. In listening work, it may be best to avoid focusing on examples where the final rise is barely audible.

e. Make connections with grammar. Although intonation is independent of grammar, there are some useful coincidences. One is that you can make a sentence sound like a question by using a rising tone – as in the phrase *A handbag?* for example. On the other hand, if you use a falling tone it will sound like a statement.

f. Make connections with discourse. For example, you can make a phrase sound incomplete with a rising tone or complete with a falling tone. See Tip 29 for more on this.

Connect intonation and context

The falling and rising tones of English have meanings which depend on the context of the discourse. If you are going to teach intonation, the context needs to be made clear.

Intonation has a different kind of relationship with intelligibility from other aspects of pronunciation. It doesn't affect the meaning of individual words, but rather the meaning of whole utterances, and the way they relate to other utterances. At the most general level, according to linguist David Brazil (see below), fall **tones** are used for *proclaiming* (basically making a statement with new information) while rise (and fall-rise) tones are used for *referring* (basically talking about something that the listener already knows). But while this rule is beautifully simple to express, it's rather abstract, and hard to interpret in practice. If you're going to present intonation to learners, it's probably better to illustrate the rule in more limited contexts such as the ones below.

Finished or to be continued: In the following short dialogue, the first two lines will probably end with a rise (or a fall-rise) while the second two, with a fall. The rise shows the exchange is to be continued, the fall shows it's finished.

A: Hey, you know my friend Emma?   B: Yes?
A: She's just passed her exams.   B: Wow, that's brilliant!

Rises and falls may be used in the same way in lists. For example, in the list of subjects below, B will probably use rises (or a level tone, neither rising nor falling) for all of them except the last.

A: What subjects did she take?   B: English, history, science and maths.

Asking or checking: In the following exchange, A may use a falling tone to indicate a statement. For B, however, there are two possibilities. If the tone falls on *isn't it?* it shows the speaker is quite confident and is just checking. On the other hand, if the tone rises, it shows that the speaker doesn't know and is asking.

A: I'm from Essex.   B: That's near London, isn't it?

In fact, speaker A could have used a rising tone too. This would imply a hidden question such as *Do you know where that is?* This use of an asking tone is sometimes called *uptalk* (see Geoff Lindsey referenced below).

Certainty or doubt: In the following exchange, B uses a falling tone indicating certainty about the opinion expressed. Meanwhile, C uses a rising tone (specifically a fall-rise), showing doubt. It seems to imply that there is a hidden 'but'.

A: What do you think of my new jacket?
B: It's lovely!
C: Well, it certainly looks warm …

Sincere or non-committal: In the exchange in the previous section, speaker B probably uses an exaggerated **pitch**, starting very high, on the word *lovely*. This indicates that the speaker is enthusiastic and sincere in this opinion. A flatter pitch range would show the speaker is non-committal – being sarcastic perhaps. Learners should be aware that they could give this impression if they use a very flat intonation.

Tone units: the punctuation of speech: Apart from tones rising or falling, another aspect of intonation is phrasing – where to put the pauses in longer stretches of discourse. This is the equivalent of punctuation in writing. If your learners will need to give presentations or speeches in English, it's well worth preparing the phrasing in advance. They could for example decide where to divide their text into spoken chunks in advance, marking the pauses with a slash. You could illustrate the importance of phrasing by contrasting the intonation and meaning in sentence pairs like these:

1   It was cold. Outside, it was snowing.
2   It was cold outside. It was snowing.

Brazil, D. (1997) *The Communicative Value of Intonation in English*. Cambridge: Cambridge University Press.

Lindsey, G. (2019) *English after RP*. Palgrave Macmillan.

Integrate pronunciation with grammar and lexis

> It's not always easy to integrate pronunciation into lessons. For example, grammar and vocabulary don't often correlate with specific pronunciation features, so it can be hard to integrate these. However, there are some useful areas of overlap, and this tip gives some examples.

Let's say you would really like to focus on the difference between two **vowel** sounds in **minimal pairs** such as these: *not – note*; *want – won't*; *cost – coast*; *non – known*; *wok – woke*; *tossed – toast*. The first thing you might observe is: what a disparate selection of words this is! They are different parts of speech, and of very different levels of frequency and usefulness. It's hard to see how you might integrate even just two or three of these pairs into any kind of grammar or vocabulary lesson. How frustrating that pronunciation is so uncooperative!

It is true that there are many areas of pronunciation which are very hard to integrate into a flowing lesson about something else, and this no doubt explains why pronunciation tends to be neglected in coursebooks. However, there are some areas where the interests of **phonology**, grammar and lexis can be made to converge, and here are some examples:

1   **Grammatical word endings:** for example: When you're teaching or recycling plural endings (or possessives or 3rd person present simple verb forms) there are a number of pronunciation points you could bring in:

- /s/ versus /z/ minimal pairs such as *place – plays*.
- Impossible **consonant clusters**: we need a **vowel** sound before the final /z/ in *horses* because without it, the ending would be /sz/, which is impossible in English.
- **Assimilation** of voicing: a word which ends with an **unvoiced** sound gets the unvoiced /s/ plural (e.g. *cats*); a word which ends with a **voiced** sound gets the voiced /z/ ending (e.g. *dogs*).

(Similar points can be made about the past tense *-ed* endings.)

2 **Complex verb forms:** When you're working on complex verb forms such as perfect tenses or passives, focus on how auxiliary verbs such as *was* or *have* and pronouns such as *you* or *her* are normally weakened, with the vowel reduced to a **schwa** and **elision** of the /h/.

3 **Grammar forms with a featured phoneme:** When you're teaching forms with *will*, structures with *would*, or past forms with *was* and *were*, this might be a good opportunity to focus on the **phoneme** /w/ if this is problematic for your learners. Similarly, you might want to focus on /ŋ/ when teaching continuous aspects.

4 **Noun phrases:** Focus on the way that **function words** such as *a*, *and*, *the*, *of* and *some* are pronounced weakly in noun phrases such as *a piece of cake*, giving the phrase a characteristic rhythm (oOoO in this example).

5 **Clauses:** Focus on typical intonation patterns in grammatical forms with more than one clause. For example, in conditionals, the **tone** often goes up at the end of the *if* clause and down at the end of the other one.

6 **Phrasal verbs:** Focus on the **consonant** to vowel linking you often find in phrasal verbs, for example *find‿out*; *moved‿in*; *woke‿up*. Because of the linking, these may sound like *fine doubt*, *move din* and *woe cup*.

7 **Word building:** If you are teaching about how longer words can be formed by adding prefixes and suffixes, it's natural to focus on **word stress**. Some suffixes such as *-ion*, *-ic* and *-ity* attract the stress to the syllable before them, for example. This means that learners can predict with some confidence the stress in words like *competition*, *artistic* and *personality*.

8 **Compound nouns:** Focus on word stress in compound nouns. For example, contrast the stress pattern of *green house* (two separate words with the pattern OO) and *greenhouse* (one compound word with the pattern Oo).

9 **Lexical sets with a featured phoneme:** Some lexical sets happen to contain many examples of a given phoneme. If you are teaching this vocabulary, it makes sense to focus on the phoneme. For example, the name of many languages and nationalities end with /ʃ/ (e.g. *Polish*), and most ordinal numbers end with /θ/ (e.g. *fifth*).

We often think of pronunciation being about speaking, but much of what we do is perhaps more for the purpose of improving listening. Traditional approaches to listening often test it rather than teach it, and a pronunciation focus can help to remedy this.

Richard Cauldwell argues that the models of English we use for productive and receptive purposes must be different. He uses a metaphor of three forms: 'greenhouse' – speech with each word pronounced very clearly; 'garden' – connected speech, including features like **elision**, **assimilation** and **weak forms** (see Tip 26); 'jungle' – spontaneous speech including heavily eroded words and phrases such as *ashy* for *actually*. Where the focus is on production, the model can be greenhouse and perhaps garden English. However, where the focus is on listening, we must also tackle the jungle.

Traditional listening lessons often involve pre-teaching vocabulary, listening to a text and answering comprehension questions. And if the learner gets anything wrong, there isn't much to be done about it except maybe listen again. This seems to be *testing* listening rather than *teaching* it. We need to supplement the listening comprehension approach with activities which focus much more closely on the jungle of speech, and how the learner can learn to decipher it. That's the intended purpose of the suggestions which follow.

1 Ask learners to reflect on an audio they've just listened to by reading the audioscript and underlining any segments or phrases which they didn't understand during the listening. Discuss these as a class. If learners are reluctant to admit their odd transcriptions, you could set the tone by giving an example of a bit that you yourself could not quite catch when you listened. One thing you may discover with this activity is that it is often common words and phrases that learners miss (like **function words** and *actually*, for example), rather than difficult new vocabulary.

2 Play back very short segments of the audio which are hard to decode. For example, speakers often bolt through vague language like the following very quickly: *and I was kind of like, you know...* . Play the short segment over and over in quick succession if your audio device allows this. Alternatively, say it yourself, matching the way it was said in the audio. If possible, slow it down but keep the same distortions as the full speed version. This allows learners to discover some of the ways that words get distorted in the jungle. They may also take away this insight: the segments of speech which are most unclear and accelerated are often those which don't contain crucial information, so don't give up listening when you encounter them.

3 Make your own questions to go with the audio but design the items with a close focus on the pronunciation rather than on general comprehension. For example, for a specific segment of the audio, design a multiple-choice type question where the learners have to identify which phrase they heard from a number of plausible competing possibilities, for example:

a. *they weren't on the stand; b. they won't understand; c. they worked in the sand; d they weren't told to stand.*

4 Do dictation exercises. Choose a short segment of the audio (or simply say the segments yourself) and ask the learners to listen a couple of times and then transcribe what they think they heard on a piece of paper. Take in the papers and compare what they have written. Choose some of the odd transcriptions and put them on the board, along with the original segment of text. Discuss what might be the cause of the mishearing.

5 If you are using a coursebook with audio which is obviously scripted and read out very clearly by actors, it will not be ideal for working on jungle features. In this case, you may need to bring in some more authentic audio to use in class.

Cauldwell, R. (2018) *A Syllabus for Listening – Decoding*. Birmingham: Speech in Action.

Hancock, M. and McDonald, A. (2014) *Authentic Listening Resource Pack*. Surrey: Delta Publishing.

Bring more pronunciation into a busy course

32

> Pronunciation content is often very brief and generic in coursebooks and syllabuses. In this tip, we look at ways of boosting the opportunities for pronunciation presentation and practice in a busy course.

Dear reader, do you work with a coursebook (or a course syllabus) which devotes very little attention to pronunciation? And is the scheduling so tight that there is little time left over to bring in any supplementary material? If so, I suspect you may be in the majority. So below, I would like to present six suggestions on how to modify and amplify the pronunciation content in the material you use.

1 Linger longer

When presenting a new word, don't just focus on the meaning. Linger a bit longer over the way it sounds. Encourage learners to savour the word by saying it fast and slowly, and in different voices. In a recent class, my learners agreed that the word *soothing* sounded soothing, and then competed to say it in the most soothing way possible. They also loved the way *stubborn* sounded stubborn. These words became fun and memorable for them, and pronunciation was at the heart of that.

2 Reverse the presentation

Coursebooks often have a task sequence in which new grammar is presented and practised, and at the end there is a very brief pronunciation focus which appears like an afterthought. Why not switch this around and sometimes present the pronunciation before the grammar? Take a few example sentences from the grammar section and write them on the board. Before the learners even open their books, work on the pronunciation of these sentences. Focus on sounds learners find difficult, on features of connected speech like **linking** and **elision**. Do some creative drilling (see Tip 36). Then, by the time you come to the grammar presentation, the example sentences are already familiar, three-dimensional pieces of language.

3 Tongue texts

If you are focusing on reading skills, reading aloud may not be an appropriate activity. However, many texts in coursebooks are there for language presentation rather than skills development, and reading these aloud can be beneficial, especially if there is a specific pronunciation focus. This may be as simple as making sure the punctuation is reflected in the way you say it. Or you could ask learners to prepare and rehearse, for example by underlining the key words that they want to stress.

4 Scan the script

Coursebooks often have the script of the audio material in the back of the book, and I sometimes use this for pronunciation work. Recently, for example, I noticed that the text had a lot of words where the final *t* was cut or replaced with a **glottal stop**. I asked learners to scan the script and underline pairs of words where the first word ended with a *t* and the next began with a **consonant** sound (e.g. *quite nice*). Then we focused on the pronunciation of these. This activity is also good for a focus on sound and spelling correspondences.

5 Drop and swap

Coursebooks are often made for many different countries and contexts. That means the pronunciation exercises can't be very focused. But by trying to cater for everybody, sometimes they end up catering for nobody. For example, they might give a list of words and ask learners to put them in the correct column according to a random set of **phonemes** at the tops of the columns. Maybe drop this exercise and swap it for one which focuses on the phonemes which are problematic for your specific learners. If possible, present phonemes contrastively in **minimal pairs**, so that learners can compare them.

6 Treasure the memory

The pronunciation content in unit tests and review pages is often quite minimal in coursebooks, but that doesn't mean you can't recycle it. Keep a written or mental note of pronunciation work you do, including any incidental things that emerge during lessons. Take photos of any board work you've been doing involving pronunciation. Then remember to refer to the pronunciation work or elicit it from learners at frequent intervals in later lessons. Let it become a treasured part of the collective class memory.

C: How to teach it

The tips in this section are concerned with the techniques and methods we use in the classroom – the pedagogy. We will deal with such issues as presenting patterns, providing practice and giving feedback and correction.

33

Encourage a growth mindset

> Teachers and learners often have a mindset which says that pronunciation ability is something fixed – you're either good at it or you aren't. It's more constructive to believe that we're all capable of learning if we make the effort.

When we see successful people, athletes for example, we see the results – the amazing things they can do – but not the process – the huge amount of effort behind their abilities. As a result, we are tempted to suppose that their success is a consequence of innate talent.

The belief that success is attributable to talent can lead to what psychologist Carol Dweck (see below) calls *a fixed mindset*. A person with this mindset believes that abilities are fixed: you either have the ability or you don't. If you fail at something, it simply means you don't have that ability and you might as well give up. There's no point persisting with something you're no good at because it will always end in failure.

Dweck contrasts the fixed mindset with what she calls *a growth mindset*. A person with this mindset thinks you can do just about anything if you put enough effort into it. For them, ability is not something fixed, but something which you can acquire through hard work. Trial and error are essential, so failures are a natural part of growth.

It's obvious which mindset will be more productive when it comes to pronunciation teaching and learning. Acquiring new articulation habits involves experimentation, and experiments are bound to have mixed results. If our learners try but fail, we want them to learn from this and try again. We don't want them to just give up. So we need to encourage a growth mindset, and here are a few ideas on how to go about this.

1 Focus on the process, not the result

Learners sometimes embark on pronunciation courses in the expectation of an unrealistic result such as sounding like a 'native speaker'. Their expectations are unlikely to be realised, and this can promote a fixed mindset response such as, 'I'm no good at this'. Better to focus on growth: the ongoing process of becoming more intelligible. This is something we can all realistically achieve, with a certain amount of effort, and it's actually more useful than acquiring somebody else's accent.

2 Focus on effort, not talent

Some learners seem to be able to pick up pronunciation points easily, while others struggle. For us teachers, it's tempting to think this is a question of talent – some learners have a natural gift for pronunciation, others don't. However, teachers can't do anything about 'natural gifts'. What we *can* do something about is effort. It's not just a question of encouraging the learners to make *more* effort; it's also about showing them how to focus their efforts more effectively.

3 Demand high

A fixed mindset encourages the belief that there is a single fixed finishing line, and once you have reached it, job done! This view creates a problem for class dynamics. The learners who've already passed the finishing line switch off while the rest struggle to catch up. A growth mindset encourages the belief that any learner can grow and improve, no matter what their starting level. No matter how good your learners' skills are, there are always ways in which they could develop further. The learners in your class can all be learning at the same time, but just not necessarily the same thing.

4 Give empowering feedback, not hollow praise

We teachers tend to make comments such as 'Very good!' almost like a knee-jerk response. The intention is benign, but the effect may not always be. For the learner to be empowered by the feedback, they need to know *why* their performance was good. If you need to give feedback, you could say something like this, depending on the level of the class:

'That was fine. You exaggerated the length of the **vowel**, but it was very clear.'

This tells the learner that exaggeration was an effective strategy, which is something they can learn from.

Dweck, C. (2007) *Mindset: The New Psychology of Success.* New York: Random House.

34

Build on what learners already know and feel

> You can prepare the ground for pronunciation teaching by doing classroom activities which focus not on specific features but on the sound of English (and other languages) as a whole.

It can be interesting to ask learners to speak their **L1** in the way that an English-speaking person would. One time I tried this, my Spanish learner spoke Spanish to hilarious effect, with long, drawled **vowels**, and a tongue which seemed to be curled back the whole time (as if saying an American-style /r/). This learner clearly knew things about English pronunciation that I had never taught him!

The activity described above demonstrates how learners usually have impressions and feelings about pronunciation before you even begin. They don't come empty-handed. Before you get down to the details of teaching, you can use 'holistic' activities like this to prepare the ground by finding out what the learners already know and feel about pronunciation.

By 'holistic', I mean viewing the topic of pronunciation *as a whole* rather than focusing on individual details. A holistic approach to pronunciation teaching needs not focus exclusively on the target language but may also compare it to other languages – particularly the learner's L1, of course. It may focus on the general position of the lips and jaw which native speakers of different languages tend to adopt – so-called *voice settings*. It may take into account subjective aspects of pronunciation, such as how different languages 'sound' and 'look' and our feelings and stereotypes about them.

Voice settings: When people mimic foreign **accents**, like my Spanish learner above, they tend to exaggerate the features which they find most salient. They may even 'pull a face', in other words, adopt a facial expression which they associate with that accent. What they are probably doing, by intuition, is attempting to reproduce the voice settings of the language which lies behind the accent, that is, the typical lip, tongue and jaw positions.

You can direct learners' attention to voice settings by, for example, playing videos with the sound off, and asking them to guess which language the people are speaking. Then have a class discussion about what features helped them to guess.

Perhaps the key feature of English-speakers' voice settings is the relaxedness of the articulators. There is little effort in the lip movements – a feature which contrasts strongly with French, for example. Clement Laroy (see below) suggests a fun activity to raise awareness of this: getting learners to try being ventriloquists. A ventriloquist is someone who entertains an audience by holding a puppet and speaking without visibly moving his or her mouth, so that the voice seems to come from the puppet. Your learners could just use their hand to 'do the speaking' instead of a puppet, of course.

A less visible characteristic of English voice settings is the amount of work done by the tongue tip in the area of the **alveolar ridge**. Take the sound /s/ for example, which may be created using the tongue tip in English, but the top surface of the tongue in other languages. I often point this out to learners as a point of interest and background information.

We should bear in mind that while non-English voice settings do contribute to a non-English accent, they do not necessarily damage international intelligibility. Voice settings will however be a key focus of instruction if you are in the business of accent-training – working with actors, for instance.

Subjective aspects: We can get at learners' subjective feelings about the sound of English and other languages by asking directly. For example, ask them to list five languages which they've heard being spoken and compare them: which do they prefer and why? Alternatively, you can use more indirect and imaginative approaches involving similes. For example, use questions like these:

What is the sound of English like to you? Choose the best answer.

1   a. It's smooth like a peach. b. It's rough like a pineapple.
2   a. It's like eating milk chocolate. b. It's like eating fresh bread.
3   a. It's like flying through the clouds. b. It's like swimming in the waves.

You will find imaginative material of this kind in the book by Laroy referenced below. The indirect approach has the advantage of steering the learners away from resorting to ready-made stereotypes.

Laroy, C. (1995) *Pronunciation*. Oxford: Oxford University Press.

35

Develop a class vocabulary

> In pronunciation teaching, you need ways of referring to
> useful concepts. These may be specialist vocabulary items,
> or simple terms that you or the learners invent. But don't
> complicate matters with too many technical words.

Being able to name the controls of a car, such as *steering wheel* or
hand brake, won't help you to drive. However, it *will* help you to
communicate with your instructor – and *that* will help you to drive. A
similar point can be made for pronunciation teaching – learning words
to refer to pronunciation concepts, such as **fricative** or **unvoiced**, will
not enable your learners to pronounce the target language better, but it
will help in the process of learning.

We need words to refer to pronunciation concepts, but they don't
necessarily have to be the 'official' terms. After all, the learners only
need these terms as a temporary learning tool; they are not the learning
objective in themselves. I usually avoid complex-sounding technical
terms such as **alveolar ridge** or *affricate* – using such words seems
like an unnecessary distraction, and they aren't very useful outside the
learning situation of your pronunciation class. You can often create
your own words for such concepts, or invite learners to suggest a word
or phrase. For example, for *alveolar ridge*, learners might suggest *tooth
hill* or something similar in their first language.

In this tip, I mean by 'vocabulary' something wider than simply lexical
items. I mean ways of referring to things specifically developed in and
by the class. Take **vowel** sounds for example. When you demonstrate
a sound, encourage learners to play with it and make associations.
For example, for the /uː/ sound as in *food*, say the vowel by itself. Get
learners to say it as if they are reacting to a nice surprise – *oooh!* After
that, you can refer to it as the 'surprise vowel'. This mental association
between the sound and an image gives it a kind of personality and
makes it memorable. Once learners have the idea, encourage them to

suggest images for other vowel sounds, and these can then become a 'class vocabulary' which you can use again whenever you refer to those sounds. But more than just points of reference, these associations come to be something like class in-jokes.

Your class vocabulary need not be only verbal; it can include body language and gestures too. I often reinforce the idea of **contrastive stress** using a dramatic rise of my eyebrows to coincide with the stressed word and encourage learners to do the same. Or to talk about what happens to the *t* in *must*, I hold out a pen at arm's length and open my fingers so that it drops to the floor, explaining that the *t* is dropped. This action eventually becomes a gesture which learners immediately understand to mean *elision*.

Think twice before introducing new metalanguage (vocabulary about language). In the pronunciation class, there is some which is very helpful, and which you will use again and again. However, there is also some metalanguage which I've rarely found any need for in my classes – examples include *minimal pair*, *homophone* and *diphthong*. I mentioned above that you may use less technical sounding alternatives, but for some things you may not need any words at all. There's no need to clutter your toolbox with tools you don't need.

Finally, beware of false friends from outside the realm of pronunciation. Examples which readily spring to mind are *vowel*, **consonant** and *syllable*. I've found that whenever I first use the term *vowel* or even *vowel sound*, learners will assume I mean the five vowel letters of the alphabet rather than the **phonemes**. Make sure you get that clarified before you get too far into the lesson. For example, if you have a phonemic chart on the wall, point at the symbols in the vowel area of the chart – there are many more than five!

36   Be mindful about drilling

> **Drilling does not enjoy a good reputation in English teaching, because it can seem dull and mindless. However, it's extremely useful in pronunciation teaching, especially if we are mindful in the way we use it.**

The verb *drill* has something of the 'mindless' connotation associated with military parade formation. Perhaps for this reason, the technique of drilling in the language classroom developed a bad reputation during the growth of the communicative approach. That's a pity, because it's a very useful activity, especially for pronunciation purposes.

What I would like to suggest, in this tip, is that we make full use of drilling in pronunciation teaching, but try to be mindful about it. Let's look at it by way of answering three questions: why, what and how should we drill?

Why should we drill?

Drilling has traditionally been used in language teaching to help learners remember things. However, in the specific case of pronunciation, I think this is more about muscle memory than anything more cognitive. It's about getting the muscles of the articulators familiar with the necessary movements. It's mouth-gym.

Equally important are the connections between mouth and ear. While we are adjusting what we do with our mouths, we simultaneously hear the result of our efforts. Muscle memory and auditory memory are mutually reinforcing. Drilling is as important for listening as for speaking. For that reason, I think it's worth drilling features which the learner needs receptively, such as connected speech, even if these are not needed for intelligibility in their production.

What should we drill?

We can drill just about any aspect of pronunciation, and do it mindfully. The main point is that you can vary the size of the chunks that you drill – it doesn't have to be just words or full sentences. Here are two example activities, one on individual sounds and one on connected speech.

1 **Sound-morphing:** Produce a sound (for example the *th* sound /θ/), but elongated. Get the class to join in. Then, without stopping, change it to another nearby sound (for example /s/) and get the class to follow. You may want to point at the sounds on the chart as you do this. Then repeat, but ask the class to focus their minds on how their mouth position changes as they move from one sound to the other.

2 **Looping-the-links:** Choose a very small linked up fragment which learners are finding tricky (for example, *that'd be good*) and repeat it over and over in a loop, getting the class to join in. Note that it starts to sound weird after a few loops, which is good because it focuses the learners' mind on the sound rather than the meaning. Afterwards, you could ask the learners if they noticed anything strange about the way it sounded. They may for example notice that the *d* of *that'd* sounded like a /b/.

How should we drill it?

You can experiment with different participation formats. Typically, you will model the chunk, or play an audio of the chunk, and the whole class repeats it. Alternatively, selected individuals may repeat it. Don't insist that the learners speak out loud straight away if they feel too self-conscious to do so. It's still good practice even if they only sub-vocalise it to themselves to begin with.

It may be possible to get a selected learner to be the model, instead of you or the audio, if someone in the class is particularly good at the phrase you're working on. If you are using a more extended drill text, such as a rap or chant (see Tip 43 for an example), you could divide the class into two teams. One team models each line of the rap and the other repeats it like an echo. Then the teams swap roles.

Whichever format you are using, listen for trouble. If it's clear that some members of the class are having difficulty repeating the chunk, work on it more slowly and, if possible, discuss what the difficulty is.

37 Focus on the physical

> There is a very physical aspect to pronunciation, so it is appropriate to use classroom techniques which focus on the physical production of speech. Here we will see some examples of these kinds of activities.

Among the various aspects of language we need to focus on in class, pronunciation is unique. Things like grammar and vocabulary are essentially cognitive, but pronunciation is also very physical. This is part of what makes it potentially so appealing: it can offer a change of focus in a class which is becoming a bit too 'heads down'.

As a pronunciation teacher, you will want to start collecting 'tricks of the trade'. You will find these in many of the resource books which have been written about teaching pronunciation. The kind of tricks I'm referring to are what phonetics expert John Catford describes as 'experiments': activities you can do which help to make you more aware of the physical movements of your own articulatory organs.

Although Catford's experiments are for students of phonetics, you can use similar ones with your learners. These will give them a kind of 'hands on' experience which can be instructive and memorable. In the list below, you will find a collection of examples of how we can focus on the physical in this way. For each one, the purpose is given first, followed by the kind of instruction you might give to the learner. Be aware though that some learners may be uncomfortable about doing some of these experiments for cultural or personal reasons.

To compare **unvoiced** and **voiced** pairs like /s/ and /z/: Put your fingers in your ears and say the sounds. You'll hear and feel a loud vibration for the /z/ but not for the /s/.

To compare **aspirated** and unaspirated pairs like /p/ and /b/: Hold a tissue paper in front of your mouth and say the sounds. The paper will blow out for /p/ but not for /b/.

To compare **stop** and **fricative** pairs like /t/ and /s/: Try to extend the sound as long as possible. You can make the /s/ as long as you want, but the /t/ can only be short.

To prove that the sound in **nasal consonants** comes from the nose: Say an extended sound /m/, then pinch your nose. The sound will stop.

To show the tongue position, for example in the sound /k/: Try to say the sound when you're breathing in rather than out. Your tongue will feel cold where it touches the roof of the mouth.

To check the teeth, tongue and lip positions in sounds like /θ/: Switch your phone to selfie mode and use it as a mirror. Say /θ/ and check you can see your tongue touching your top teeth.

To show the forward or backward position of the tongue in **vowels** like /iː/ and /uː/: Make an extended *eeeee* sound and then change it to *ooooo*. Repeat, but with a pencil touching the end of your tongue. The pencil will go further into your mouth.

To compare **tense** (long) vowels like /iː/ and **lax** (short) vowels like /ɪ/: Put an elastic band between finger and thumb. Move the finger and thumb apart as you say the long vowel and together for the short one. You'll feel the tension and slack in the elastic band.

To compare jaw position in closed vowels like /iː/ and open vowels like /ɑː/: Put your finger on your nose and thumb on your chin. Say the two sounds. Notice how your finger and thumb move apart.

To raise awareness of lip position for different sounds: Work with a partner. Say words from a list in random order, but silently. Your partner must identify the word.

To make sure that emphasis is noticeable in **tonic stress**: Raise your eyebrows and/or make expressive hand gestures at the same time as you say the part of the sentence which has stress.

To differentiate strong and weak syllables in rhymes and chants: Clap or tap a regular beat and say the rhyme or chant, making sure that the strong syllables happen at the same moment as the clap.

Catford, J. C. (2001) *A Practical Introduction to Phonetics*. Oxford: Oxford University Press.

38 Encourage cognitive engagement

A key part of teaching is keeping the class mentally engaged with the subject matter. This is just as true for pronunciation teaching as other areas of the curriculum.

Read the (short) conversation below and decide who is speaking and where:

T: How do you pronounce the past of *read*? (Initiation)
L: /red/! (Response)
T: Yes, good. (Feedback)

No prizes for guessing it's an exchange between a teacher and learner in a language class. This is a conversational pattern which is very common in classrooms generally, and it's been called *The IRF pattern*, with the letters standing for *initiation, response* and *feedback*.

I'm sure most of us teachers will find ourselves talking this way from time to time, but why do we do it? I think the answer is that we're trying to check that the learners are 'with' us, mentally. The basic idea is a good one – we need to encourage cognitive engagement. However, there is a danger in relying solely on the IRF for this purpose: it can feel rather routine and mechanical if overused. Let's have a look at some variations and alternatives. The titles of the sections below refer to what the learners are doing.

Answering questions: This is basically what the learners are doing in the IRF pattern above, but I like to break the routine sometimes by modifying the 'moves'. For example, try changing the 'feedback' move: instead of giving your evaluation, keep a straight face and ask, 'Are you sure?' Or ask another learner, 'Do you agree with that?' You can also play with the 'initiation' move. Ask a question with no answer like, 'What's the difference in pronunciation between past tense *read* and the colour *red*?' Or break the rules completely by asking a 'real' question – one that you don't know the answer to, such as 'Has anyone read a good book lately?'

Noticing: The question in the conversation above is essentially a way of directing learners' attention. That's **OK**, but it's slightly coercive. It's better if something grabs learner attention without the explicit 'initiation' move. For example, you could set the learners a puzzle to solve such as this riddle: 'What's black, white and /red/ from beginning to end?' (answer = a book)

Identifying patterns: You can encourage cognitive engagement in the tasks that you give learners. For example, write the words below on the board:

> *heat, peace, meat, mean, great, eat*

Ask learners to find the pattern and one word which breaks the pattern. (The pattern is that *ea* is pronounced /iː/, and *great* breaks the pattern.)

Finding connections: Challenge learners to find connections between two things which appear to be very different. For example, ask them what sounds the following pairs of words have in common:

> *quickly – wine* (answer = /w/)
> *holiday – wash* (answer = /ɒ/)
> *night – buying* (answer = /aɪ/)

Finding reasons: Present learners with strange pronunciation facts and ask them to suggest explanations. For example: 'You often see the contractions *she's, it's* and *that's*, but never *this's*. What do you think is the reason for this?' (Because it's very difficult to say two /s/ together.)

Solving puzzles: Problems get more complex if the question involves more stages. Here's an example: 'If you have a very bad cold and you say the word *may*, it sounds like *bay*. Why?' (When you say /m/, the lips are closed and the sound comes from the nose. When you have a cold, the nose is blocked. It comes out as /b/ because this sound is also made with the lips closed.)

Being inquisitive: In the IRF pattern above, it's always the teacher who initiates. Try to encourage learners to be inquisitive about language, and initiate questions for themselves instead. A class atmosphere where learners feel inclined to ask questions is something that will take time to achieve. I think the way to get started is to ask more open questions such as 'What do you think is the reason for this spelling?' or 'Why do you think it's pronounced that way?'

Learners can pick up some patterns of pronunciation intuitively. However, there are some which you can present explicitly to speed the learning process along.

We can identify patterns in the pronunciation of English at three different levels – sound-level, word-level and conversation-level, and we will look at each of these in turn below.

Sound-level patterns

Sounds which are too alike do not make easy neighbours. Try saying *an apple* without the *n*: it's hard. We need the *n* to keep the similar **vowels** separate. The same thing happens with **consonants**. Say *Smith's* and *Jones's*. The *s* is happy enough to come straight after the *th* in *Smith's*, but it's not happy after the *s* in *Jones's*, and we have to insert a vowel sound to separate them. Some learners may pick up 'rules' like this intuitively; others may learn them more efficiently with explicit teaching.

When two sounds live side by side, one of them may change in order to be more like its neighbour in some way. Compare the final *s* in *wife's* and *wives*, for example. The first is pronounced /s/ so that it's **unvoiced** to match the /f/ before it. The second is pronounced /z/ so that it's **voiced** to match the preceding /v/.

Sounds may also try to match the mouth position of a neighbour. For example, in the combination *np*, the *n* may become /m/ to match the lips-together position of the following *p*. You can hear this in the word *signpost* for instance. Again, many learners will pick up these rules intuitively, but sometimes explicit awareness can help.

Some sounds are happy together in one place but can't stand being together in others. For example, in English, *s* is fine after *p* at the end of a syllable (for example, *tops*), but it refuses to come after *p* at the beginning. In words like *psychic* for example, the *p* stays silent. However, other languages don't always play by the same rules – Greek and Polish have no problem with this syllable-initial *ps*. Awareness of such differences between the rules of their own language and English can be very useful for learners. These kinds of rules are known as *phonotactics.*

Word-level patterns

If the rules in the last section relate to the physical abilities of the mouth, the patterns in this section are set purely by convention. They are spelling patterns and **word stress** patterns.

We sometimes point out to learners that English spelling is not **phonetic.** However, it's best not to overstate the case: the idea that spelling is total anarchy is neither helpful nor motivating. In fact, there are lots of patterns, and some of them are easy enough to present explicitly in your lessons (see Tip 23), for example. Other patterns are perhaps better left to intuition.

Like spelling patterns, word stress patterns are not categorical. You can't say, for example, that all two-syllable nouns have the stress on the first syllable; you can only say that *most* of them do. However, as long as we make this clear, I think that some patterns are eminently teachable (see Tip 24, for example). Nevertheless, there is no doubt that word stress is mostly something that learners need to commit to memory on a word-by-word basis.

Conversation-level rules

The first pattern I would mention here relates to rhythm. I think it's useful to raise our learners' awareness of the distinction between **content words** and **function words,** because the former tend to be pronounced strongly and the latter weakly (see Tip 25 for more on this). This pattern of strong and weak is useful because it forms the baseline for intonation rules and, in particular, **tonic stress** (sometimes known as 'sentence stress').

The basic rule of tonic stress is that you put the stress on the last content word in a sentence or phrase. For example, in *What did you think of it?* the stress would be on *think.* However, this is a very different kind of rule from the ones above: it's made to be broken. You can *choose* to put the stress on any word in the phrase in order to create a specific meaning. But you need to know the rule in order to break it meaningfully. See Tip 27 for more on this.

> It's good for learners to practise pronunciation in
> communication activities where a successful outcome
> depends on their pronunciation accuracy. These kinds of
> activities tend to be based on the minimal pair principle.

I think it's important to remind our learners (and ourselves) of the
practical purpose of pronunciation as frequently as possible, and this is
where communication activities come in: they demonstrate pronunciation
in action. If you tell someone that you need to *save*, and they hand you
a razor (so that you can *shave*), you know that the pronunciation didn't
work as you intended, and this is very powerful feedback. A classroom
communication activity can replicate this kind of experience.

If you want your communication activity to focus very specifically on
pronunciation, you need two words or phrases with a similar pronunciation
but a different meaning, so that both the speaker and listener must be
careful to distinguish them. The **minimal pair** is the obvious candidate.

A minimal pair consists of two words which differ only in one
phoneme, for example:

A. *bear*   B. *pear*

The most basic activity with a pair like this is for the speaker to say one
of the two words, and the listener to identify which one, for example
by giving the letter, or pointing at it. You can give a bit more context by
putting the words into sentences:

A. *There's a bear in that tree.*   B. *There's a pear in that tree.*

As an alternative to saying A or B, the listener could make an
appropriate response, for example: *Oh really? Shall we run away?* or
they could point at a picture, if the minimal pair is easy to illustrate.

You can extend minimal pair activities into longer game-like activities.
For example, you can make a street map in which the street names are
all minimal pairs such as *Beach Street* and *Peach Street*. Learners mark

a few places on the map and then explain to their partners where they are, for example: 'It's on the corner of Beach Street and Pear Road.'

Another example is a class roll call. Give each learner a card with their new name on it. The names are all similar, for example: *Jay Bart, Jane Burt, G. Burt,* and so on. Then call out each name and the learner with that name replies, 'Here!'

There are other kinds of pronunciation pairs which are not strictly speaking minimal pairs, but which you can also do the same kinds of activities with.

One of the words in the pair has a phoneme which is missing in the other, for example:

A. *hair*   B. *air,*   A. *gold*   B. *goal,*   A. *support*   B. *sport,*
A. *ten*   B. *tenth,*   A. *ask*   B. *asked*

These are pairs of phrases which differ only very slightly:

A. *Alice is here*   B. *Alice was here,*   A. *I like to cook*   B. *I like the cook*

There aren't many pairs of words or phrases which are distinguished exclusively by the word stress. There are some, however, for example:

A. *REcord*   B. *recORD,*   A. *GREENhouse*   B. *green HOUSE*

The pairs below are distinguishable only by the phrasing, which reflects the punctuation:

A. *They're leaving. Soon it'll be quieter.*
B. *They're leaving soon. It'll be quieter.*

A. *Who said 'Martin'?*   B. *'Who?' said Martin.*
A. *Let's eat, Grandma!*   B. *Let's eat Grandma!*

You can also make pairs which differ only in terms of the **tonic stress** or **tone**. In the examples below, the words or phrases are responses to the statements in brackets:

A. *South AFRICA* (Where are you from?)
B. *SOUTH Africa* (Which part of Africa are you from?)

A. *What?* (I've got some bad news for you.)
B. *What!* (I'm afraid your house has burnt down.)

Hancock, M. (2017) *PronPack 3: Pronunciation Pairworks,* Chester: Hancock McDonald ELT.

> Games and puzzles work well for raising awareness of rules
> and patterns in pronunciation. These kinds of activity are
> usually based on a few very simple principles.

My favourite kind of pronunciation puzzle is the maze. This consists of
a grid of 'rooms' containing words connected by 'doorways'. The learner
has to find a route from top left to bottom right, and they can only go
through a room if the word in it has a given feature – for example, a
certain **phoneme** or stress pattern. (See an example in Appendix 4.) I first
presented this type of activity in *Pronunciation Games*, published in 1995.

I've reflected on this activity over the years. Learners tend to say the
words to themselves as they work through a maze, but there's nothing
to stop them completing it in silence. So in that case, are mazes really
a 'pronunciation' activity? Can 'pronunciation' be silent? I've come to
the conclusion that the answer is yes: part of pronunciation is physical
and not silent, but another part of it is quietly cerebral. This latter part
relates to the rules and patterns outlined in Tip 39, and these patterns
are the focus of the example activities suggested below.

Since these activities are presented to learners in a printed form, we
need to make sure that the spelling doesn't 'give the game away'. For
example, the phoneme /m/ nearly always corresponds to the letter 'm'.
Consequently, there's no challenge whatsoever in Question 1 below.
Question 2 on the other hand is interesting, because the relationship
between /s/ and the spelling is not so obvious.

1   Which word does not contain /m/: *calm, market, anybody,
    something, comma*?
2   Which word does not contain /s/: *save, rice, box, grapes, roses, pass*?

Odd one out

Questions 1 and 2 above are based on the odd-one-out principle. The
learner is challenged to find the word which breaks the pattern in some
way. This works well for sounds as well as **word stress** patterns.

Matching

Question 3 below is based on a matching principle: there are pairs of words which have something in common hidden within lists of words. In this example, learners cannot guess from the spelling because the vowel in all the words is spelt *ea*.

3   Match each word from List a with a word from List b. The two words must contain the same **vowel** sound.

   a. *break, bean, bread, learn, wear*
   b. *earn, head, great, bear, heat*

Note that the matching principle can also be used in card games. The players each have a pack of cards with words on them and take turns to place them face up on the table. If two cards with matching vowel sounds occur together, the first player to notice this wins all the cards on the table.

Classifying

In this kind of activity, learners have to classify words from a list according to a pronunciation feature. In Question 4 below, this feature is the pronunciation of the *-ed* ending of past tense verbs.

4   Add these words below to the correct list, a–c:
   walked, called, wanted, needed, closed, stopped

   a. *-ed* = /t/   b. *-ed* = /d/   c. *-ed* = /ɪd/

The classifying principle is sometimes used in board and dice games.

Common feature

The maze activity described above is based on the idea that all of the words in the correct route share a common feature. For example, all of the words in the maze may contain nouns with two syllables, and learners can only go through a 'room' if the word has the stress on the first syllable (for example, *melon, salad, coffee, lemon …*). Note that some of the rooms will contain distractors – in this case, words which have the stress on the second syllable (for example, *dessert, machine, hotel …*). You can't pass through these rooms.

Hancock, M. (1995) *Pronunciation Games*. Cambridge: Cambridge University Press.

For aspects of pronunciation which are very dependent on context, drama and role-play may be the best kind of classroom practice. Such activities are especially useful for sentence stress and intonation.

Read the dialogue below. I think it's fair to say that B is annoyed.

A: *You weren't listening to me.*　B: *I WAS listening!*

If you wanted to elicit this kind of language in the classroom authentically, you would need to get the learners to annoy each another – which would be counter-productive, to say the least! That's why we need drama and role-play in the classroom – so that we can bring in reality without it needing to be *too* real.

In the specific context of pronunciation teaching, drama and role-play become particularly useful when it comes to practising intonation. Intonation is entirely context-dependent, and drama can supply that context. In order to practise intonation in the classroom, learners will have to imagine themselves to be in different situations.

Authentic scripts are good for receptive skills but invented scripts may be better for production. The advantage of authentic scripts is realism, helping to bridge the gap from classroom to the outside world. The disadvantage is that they don't provide a lot of examples of the target feature that you wish to focus on, and it can be difficult to work out what was going on if you weren't there yourself.

An invented script can be written to include good examples of the target feature in the briefest possible space, and the contexts can be made simpler and more obvious. For example, the context could be the argumentative couple that we saw in the mini-dialogue at the top of the page, contradicting each other – a great context for **contrastive stress**.

A good intonation activity is for learners to try saying a single word, but with different attitudes. The other learner just listens and tries to identify the attitude. For example, the activity could be to say the word *really* as if you are annoyed, afraid, suspicious etc. or to say *hello* as if to the president, a police officer, your best friend, etc.

In order to focus on intonation without distraction, we can ask learners to dramatise dialogues in which each speaker only uses one word at a time. For example:

A: *Quick!*   B: *What?*   A: *Bus!*   B: *Bus?*   A: *Bus.*   B: *Why?*
A: *Leaving!*   B: *Now?* ...

Role-plays involve dramatising, but without a script. The learners have to imagine they are different characters. These can be chosen to create opportunities to practise a pronunciation feature such as contrastive stress. For example, learners in pairs imagine they are argumentative siblings. Everything A says, B disagrees with and vice versa. They might start like this:

A: *I think football's the most exciting sport to watch.*
B: *No way! Football's the WORST sport to watch!*
A: *What do YOU like, then?*

Alternatively, the learners can be themselves, but they have to imagine they are in a different situation. For example, they are trying to fix a meeting with each other over the phone, but the reception is very poor:

A: *Let's meet at five o'clock on Thursday.*
B: *Nine o'clock's a bit late for me ...*
A: *No, not NINE o'clock, FIVE o'clock.*

Rather than create dialogues to highlight specific pronunciation points, you can go the opposite way and be more opportunistic. Find short drama scripts which already exist (see, for example, *The Drama Book*) and scan the text to see what opportunities are there for pronunciation work.

As well as being valuable for learning, drama can be motivating. Speaking in role can help learners to overcome embarrassment. For example, learners may feel embarrassed to use English-sounding intonation. However, if they have a role to 'hide' behind, they can practise without feeling that it reflects badly on their own true selves.

Savage, A. (2019) *The Drama Book*. Branford: Alphabet Publishing.

43   Use chants and rhymes

> Chants, rhymes, songs and raps can be very valuable
> sources of pronunciation practice. Here, we look at what
> they can be used for, and why.

I think that songs, and other kinds of playful texts like chants and
rhymes, have great value in pronunciation teaching, and here are three
good reasons why:

1   They're memorable

You'll find that if you've worked with a chant or rhyme or rap
thoroughly one week, the learners can often recite much of it from
memory the following week. If you did it near the end of the class, some
learners will have walked home with it playing in a loop in their heads,
doing homework you never asked of them.

2   They're built out of pronunciation

The kind of word play you find in these kinds of texts depends on the
sound of the language. Rhyming words for example are words which
share the same final **vowel** and **consonant phonemes**. Chants exploit
the syllable structure of phrases to create patterns. In other words, such
texts are built out of the very material that we're trying to teach. This is
a happy coincidence. The fact that these features are so salient in chants
and rhymes draws the learners' attention to them.

3   They're repeatable

People normally tire very quickly of something which is too repetitious.
You wouldn't want to listen to the same news bulletin five times.
However, it seems we're much more tolerant in the case of things like
songs, chants and rhymes – we can listen to these repeatedly. This is
ideal for pronunciation work, which usually requires quite a lot of
repetition. Drilling sentences is work; drilling a rap is fun.

Here's an example of a rap which I wrote for *PronPack 4*, followed by
the stages of a possible classroom activity for it. The beat falls on the
bolded words.

*You **won't** get **fit** just **sitting** on a **seat***
*If you **wanna** get **fit**, gotta **get** up on your **feet***
*Don't **fill** that **seat**, gotta **move** a little **bit***
*Kick your **feet** to the **beat**, feel the **heat**, that's **it!***

1 Give out the text with some gaps. Say the rap and ask learners to complete it.
2 Read out each line fairly slowly and ask the class to repeat it, like an echo of you.
3 Repeat shorter segments that they seem to have difficulty with, such as *sitting on a seat*, three or four times in quick succession and ask the class to repeat.
4 Get the class to clap a regular beat and lead them in saying the chant together, keeping to that rhythm.

This text has a narrow focus on the **minimal pairs**: *sit – seat*, *fit – feet* and *bit – beat*. When they recite the rap, learners can practise articulating these words. When the rap goes around in their inner ear, they get to hear them repeatedly.

The text also has a broad focus on rhythm and connected speech: **linking, weak forms, elision** and so on. Although for intelligibility, learners don't need to import these features into their normal speech, they need to be able to understand them receptively, and the rap format helps to make them noticeable and fix them in the mind.

If you're using a coursebook for young learners, the chances are that the book will already contain plenty of songs, chants and rhymes, which is great. Books for older learners don't usually include such material, in which case you'll need to look outside the book.

When searching for 'authentic' songs, chants and rhymes to use, it's difficult to find them with a narrow focus on specific phonemes like the example above. However, the good news is that most will be exploitable for the broad focus. If you're using a song, listen to it a few times before class and identify any features you may want to highlight. If you've found a rhyme you want to use, try saying it over and over to yourself and identify any useful pronunciation tips you could pick up from it.

Hancock, M. (2017) *PronPack 4: Pronunciation Poems*. Chester: Hancock McDonald ELT.

44

Give informative feedback

> Learners naturally appreciate feedback on their
> pronunciation. Try to make your feedback useful and
> informative.

When we put effort into doing something, we like to get feedback. And
it's undeniably nice when the feedback is good. But when your teacher
just says, 'Good!' after everything you say, you begin to doubt their
sincerity. Good how? You begin to thirst for something a little more
informative. Let's take a look at what it means to give informative
feedback.

Conform versus inform

Some feedback encourages learners to conform:

L: *I don't like pears.*   T: *OK, but we say 'pears'.*   L: *'Pears'?*
T: *'Pears'. Yes, good.*

In this exchange, the learner *conforms* to the teacher's way of saying the
word. However, the feedback may not have done much to *inform* the
learner. What more could have been said?

The importance of diagnosis

We can't hear the conversation above, nor see the exact context, but I'm
guessing that the learner pronounced *pears* like *peers*. My first diagnosis
would be that the learner has been misled by the spelling. It would be
perfectly reasonable to suppose that *pear* would rhyme with words like *ear,
hear, near, fear, clear,* and so on. It's a case of over-generalising a spelling
pattern. In that case, it might be worth mentioning that *pear* is exceptional,
otherwise this feedback might cause the learner to doubt the pattern.

Focused feedback

Let's suppose that the teacher in the conversation above has an **accent**
in which *r* is not pronounced in words like *pear* – an English accent,
for example. When the teacher models *pears*, the learner might think
the lack of *r* is an essential part of the correct pronunciation. You might

need to point out that it's only the **vowel** sound that you want the learner to focus on in this instance; the *r* is not a problem either way.

Feedback by result

A good form of feedback on pronunciation is to remain silent and write on the board what you understood the learner to have said. For example, they mispronounce *pear* and you write up *peer*. The learners can keep modifying their pronunciation until you write *pear*, which is the result they intended. Learners can also get this kind of feedback from the speech recognition function on their own mobile phones (see Tip 48).

More than one way of being 'correct'

I've had learners ask about the pronunciation of *either*: is the first vowel like the vowel in *bee*, or like *eye*? They find it a little disappointing to discover that both are perfectly correct. I think we feel that 'correct' means there's only *one* valid way of saying something. Let's take a different example: *tomato*. Is the second vowel sound like the vowel in *calm* or in *say*? In this instance, the first is typical in British English and the second in American – and of course, both are 'correct'. In fact, you can say most things in more than one way and yet still be intelligible. Feedback should take account of this fact.

Feedback doesn't have to be evaluative

You can give feedback to learners which is informative but not evaluative. For example: 'You're pronouncing it differently from me, but it's fine, people will understand you.' That leaves it up to the learner whether they would like to sound like you or not. Sometimes, just comparing the way we pronounce things is the only feedback we need: it satisfies the craving without being an insincere 'Good!'

Where 'correct' is correct

There is one area of pronunciation where I think the term 'correct' is entirely appropriate, and this is for the relationship between sound and spelling. Returning to the conversation at the beginning of this tip for example: let's imagine that the learner pronounces *pear* like *peer*, but has no problem with the vowel in *hair*. In that case, we know the learner _can_ say the vowel in *pear*. This is not a matter of **accent**; they're simply decoding the spelling incorrectly.

45 Control your correction reflex

> Teachers are hard-wired to respond to learners' errors by correcting them. That's fine, but we should be mindful about whether and how we do this.

Ask someone to sit with one leg crossed over the other. Then tap the person's knee and what happens? You get the well-known knee-jerk reaction: the lower leg kicks forward without the permission of its owner. Sometimes, I think we pronunciation teachers tend to correct learners as a kind of reflex reaction. Perhaps we should be more mindful, by considering questions such as these:

1 Is the 'error' really a problem?

Just because something is non-standard, that doesn't mean it's necessarily a problem for intelligibility. For example, many Australian speakers say *day* like **RP** *die* but are nevertheless intelligible. Similarly, many of the things your learners say may be non-standard but not unintelligible. It's worth bearing this in mind.

2 Is this just something that irritates me personally?

From time to time, we can easily get annoyed by some aspect of our learners' pronunciation. We say things like, 'My learners always say ... and it sounds really awful!' Whether or not the pronunciation feature is in fact problematic in terms of intelligibility, I don't think it's wise to let our own subjective dislike of it cloud our judgement. Irritation is rarely constructive.

3 Is this the right moment?

It's often good to give your feedback as soon as you notice a problem. However, sometimes it can be an unwelcome distraction. If your learner is trying to concentrate their attention on A, it might be damaging to force their attention on B. Sometimes it's better to let something pass, or make a mental note and return to it later.

4 Is this a slip or a systematic problem?

Sometimes, in the heat of a communicative interaction, a learner will make a pronunciation slip that they are perfectly capable of self-correcting. If you think an error is a slip rather than a systematic problem, you may deal with it lightly or not at all.

5 Is this an awareness or an articulation issue?

If a learner pronounces the *w* in *sword*, that's probably because they aren't *aware* that it should be silent. If a learner says *ooman* for *woman*, it's probably because they have difficulty articulating the /w/. Your feedback should be different in either case.

6 Shall I correct explicitly?

If a learner makes an error in the course of a conversation, you may correct explicitly or subtly. For example, let's say the learner talks about a man who found a sword, but pronounces the *w*. You might say, 'Actually, the *w* is silent in *sword*', or you might say, 'Oh, he found a sword, did he?' (pronouncing *sword* correctly). You have that choice.

7 Should I expand this into a mini-presentation?

You can make a quick correction in passing, or give a more complete explanation. For example, if your learner pronounces *walked* as *walkid*, you may just need to make a quick correction, or you may be tempted to go into a full mini-presentation about *-ed* endings. I used the word 'tempted' because many of us pronunciation fans might have an urge to do this – but it's not *always* advisable to give in to temptation!

8 Would this be a good opportunity for peer feedback?

One final question that's worth considering is this: might the feedback be better coming from one of the learner's classmates? It's not a good dynamic for you to be the only person in the room with all the answers. It's better for the wisdom to be more evenly distributed. Plus feedback from peers is sometimes expressed in a way that the learner can better understand. And last but not least, the learner who is giving the feedback consolidates their own ability by doing so – and gets a bit of a motivation boost too. What's not to like?

Assessment tests can help you to decide what aspects of pronunciation to focus on, and to identify what progress the learners are making.

Here are some questions to consider when assessing pronunciation.

When should I test?

It can be useful to do a diagnostic test at the beginning of your course to get some idea of 'where the learners are at' in terms of pronunciation. The focus of such a test can be very wide. Later on in the course, you can use achievement tests to find out how the learners are progressing, and then you can focus more narrowly on the specific issues you have covered in class.

How can I get a good sample of the learners' speech?

One possibility is to use a text which contains range of potential pronunciation issues and ask the learners to read it aloud. However, read-aloud texts may elicit unnatural pronunciation and encourage spelling-induced errors. An alternative might be to record learners in pairs doing a simple speaking activity such as talking about their leisure interests. In this case, assessment is a little more difficult because the text is not controlled; you need to find the pronunciation issues where they arise naturally.

How can I assess the sample?

It can be really tricky to untangle the knot of pronunciation issues that you hear in your learners' speech. The key is to choose specific features and focus exclusively on these. For this purpose, you could make a marking sheet. This is basically a list of the features you have chosen, and space to write notes next to them. The features might be, for example, a limited number of **phonemes** and phoneme clusters. Make notes on your marking sheet while you listen to the learners, either in real time or on a recording.

How can I choose what features to focus on?

Tests should be coherent with the pronunciation aims of you and your class. For example, if you're teaching for the purpose of international intelligibility, then your assessment should reflect that fact. Don't mark down learners for not using native-like features such as **weak forms** in their own production, since these aren't essential for intelligibility. Instead, focus on features which are likely to damage intelligibility. Robin Walker (see below) has a good section on assessment including an example of an intelligibility-focused marking sheet.

How should I involve the learners?

I think we should involve the learners to the maximum. Explain exactly what you're doing and why. If you have a marking sheet, why not show it to them before they do the task so they know what to focus on? This awareness is beneficial not only in the test itself, but as a learning experience more generally. The ideal is when learners become so accustomed to marking sheets that they feel able to use one themselves. Once they can do this, they can use it to assess each other in class. Instead of pair work, put the learners in groups of three – two doing a speaking activity and the third assessing. Students can also learn to assess themselves. Ask them to make a recording, and then some time later, listen back to it with a marking sheet in hand.

How can I test other aspects of pronunciation?

The reading aloud and speaking tasks above focus on learners' productive skills. To get an idea of their listening ability and pronunciation awareness, you could use a test such as the one in my book *English Pronunciation in Use* (see below). If you are making your own, you can design test items using the principles presented in Tip 41: 'matching', 'classifying' and so on. Check that your test items test what they're supposed to test. It's all too easy, for example, to create an item intending for it to test a **vowel** phoneme, but which in fact tests awareness of sound-to-spelling correlation. Another common mistake is to create pronunciation test items which test knowledge of **phonemic symbols** rather than actual pronunciation.

Hancock, M. (2007) *English Pronunciation in Use Intermediate*. Cambridge: Cambridge University Press.

Walker, R. (2010) *Teaching the Pronunciation of English as a Lingua Franca*. Oxford: Oxford University Press.

47 Help learners to deal with misunderstandings

> No matter how good your English is, in international
> communication you will always find yourself in situations
> where there are misunderstandings from time to time.
> Learners need to be effective at dealing with these.

In international communication, misunderstandings are bound to
happen occasionally. It's natural and inevitable. What learners need
to know is this: misunderstanding is not a mistake, the mistake is
remaining in a state of misunderstanding.

If you're interacting with someone from a different language background
and you find that things aren't making much sense, you need to do
something to keep the conversation moving forward until things start
to get clear again. It's like riding a bicycle: if you stop moving forward,
the bike falls over. So what can be done? I think the solution begins with
feedback, which in turn may lead to 'negotiation of meaning'.

If your interaction is face to face, then you will probably be getting feedback
the whole time. Good communicators are active listeners. They tend to
use gestures and facial expressions to reassure the speaker that messages
are being understood. They also use what are known as *backchannel
responses* – verbal expressions like *uh-huh*, *hmm* and *right*. Encourage
learners to provide such listener feedback in activities like pair work, and
to be attentive to it from their interlocutor. You could raise awareness of
it by playing a dialogue from a video with the sound off. This focuses the
attention on body language, and it's surprisingly instructive!

When active listening begins to yield negative feedback, such as a
puzzled face or an expression such as, *Sorry?* it's time to repair the
conversation. Here are some of the things you can do to achieve this,
along with typical phrases:

Listener:
- Explain your problem (*I don't understand.*)
- Ask for repetition (*Sorry, could you say that again?*)

- Prompt a repetition of the problem word (*You saw* what?)
- Suggest a paraphrase (*What, you mean like a* credit card *or something?*)

Speaker:
- Reformulate (*The battery's flat – I mean, it has no power left in it.*)
- Spell it out (*I mean 'live' with a letter i: l-i-v-e.*)
- Repeat but more slowly and clearly (*Sorry, I'll say that again …*)

You could get learners to include repair phrases like these in pair work activities – it may seem a little artificial, but it helps to make the point.

Speakers can be on the look-out for misunderstandings caused by their own L1-induced pronunciation issues and be ready to repair when necessary. Listeners can be alert to the possibility of unusual accent features in their interlocutor and be creative in working out what they are saying. Modifying your speech and listening expectations is known as *accommodation* and is a key skill in international communication (see Tip 10).

Communication activities provide an excellent context to practise negotiating meaning in classrooms where the learners have different language backgrounds: in this context, English really is being used as a Lingua Franca. On the other hand, there's a problem in *mono*lingual classrooms because the learners may understand each other's L1 influenced English, even if it would be unintelligible for outsiders. As a teacher in this situation, you may have to 'play dumb' and pretend not to understand even when you do. Also you can use interactive listening. When playing an audio, encourage learners to raise their hand to stop the audio and ask you if they need to 'repair' their understanding. In this way, they deal with the misunderstanding rather than leave it to derail their comprehension.

Some teachers try to get around the limitations of the monolingual classroom by bringing in interlocutors from the outside world via video link. I recently saw this done by a Dutch teacher in Barcelona, who got his class interacting over the internet with his brother in Holland. There was plenty of genuine negotiation of meaning in evidence, and it provided a very realistic **ELF** learning experience for the class.

48 Use resources for teachers

Supplementary resources provide materials for teachers who don't have time to make their own, and ideas for those that do. Here, we'll look at sources of both kinds of resources.

I wouldn't wish to discourage teachers from creating their own material (see Tip 49), but I'm sure many of us spend a huge amount of time re-creating stuff that's already been created before by somebody else – 're-inventing the wheel', as the expression goes. It's worth spending a little time finding out what resources are out there for teachers of pronunciation. We'll have a look at that now, but I'll keep it rather generic – many new things may become available between me writing this and you reading it!

1 **Teaching materials:** Most coursebooks include some pronunciation content, but it tends to be minimal. See Tip 32 for more on this. You can boost the pronunciation content of your lesson with supplementary material, and there are plenty of classroom-ready materials in teachers' resource books available. These may include printable worksheets for the learners, or classroom procedures laid out recipe-style. There are also websites offering this kind of material (including my own on hancockmcdonald.com).

Coursebooks and supplementary materials often come accompanied with audio recordings to model the 'correct' pronunciation. Some teachers use these in the belief that their own pronunciation is not good enough but do reconsider this assumption. After all, English is a global Lingua Franca, and the idea of there being a single correct standard seems rather old-fashioned. Plus, the teacher's voice, live in the classroom, is often more vivid than coursebook recordings.

2 **Audio-visuals:** The easy availability of video material over the internet is perhaps the single biggest benefit of technology for pronunciation teaching. Perhaps the majority of classrooms in the world are monolingual, so that the learners are living in a bubble of people who speak with a similar **accent**. If they are ever going to become accent-tolerant participants in the global speech community, they are going to need experience of listening to different voices, and online video can

provide this. Be sure to choose speakers with a range of accents and to include non-native speakers.

The audio-visual possibilities of the internet can also be truly interactive through the use of video conferencing. For this, you'll need people who are willing to be virtual visitors to your classroom – see the example at the end of Tip 47.

3   Individualisation: Resources for learners' self-study are the focus of Tip 50. However, you may sometimes want to have 'break-out' sessions in class time. For example, in a class where the learners all have different **L1** backgrounds, you may want to give them time to work separately on their own specific pronunciation issues. For instance, your Japanese learner might work on /l/ and /r/ while your Saudi learner works on /b/ and /p/. For this purpose, you could give them the relevant pages of a resource book or tell them to use the relevant section of a pronunciation app. Get them to work together afterwards in a communication activity so that they can try out their new skills in real interaction.

For learners to get instant feedback on their own speech, you could suggest they switch the speech recognition on their phone to English, say difficult words or phrases, and see how it comes out on the screen. However, be warned: this technology is not necessarily accent-tolerant, and perfectly intelligible learner utterances can get badly mis-transcribed. You need to be around to reassure your learners in case this leads them to despair!

4   Professional development: For your own continuous professional development, there are plenty of books out there dealing with phonology and teaching pronunciation. Many of them have been referenced in the tips in this book. There are also plenty of websites and blogs with pronunciation posts.

You can usually find talks and workshops on pronunciation at conferences, and also online in the form of webinars. Some teachers' associations have special interest groups relating to pronunciation teaching. For example, IATEFL has a group called PronSIG, which I have been a member of for many years.

Last but not least, there are special interest groups on social media relating to English language teaching, where you can exchange ideas with colleagues and find out about things which are going on such as conferences and webinars.

49 Make your own materials

> By making your own materials, you can focus on precisely what your learners need, and at the same time, learn more about pronunciation yourself.

It's sometimes said that the act of giving benefits the giver as well as the receiver. In a similar way, the act of teaching can help the teacher as well as the learner. Working out how to explain something helps you to understand it better yourself. In this tip, I would like to suggest a further step along this line of thought: that materials writing helps the writer. I personally have learnt so much about pronunciation by creating pronunciation materials.

What I will do in this tip is outline the typical steps I usually take when I'm trying to create a piece of material. You can also find general guidance about writing pronunciation activities in the book referenced at the end of the tip.

1   **Decide on the pronunciation focus:** The great thing about making your own material is you can focus on precisely what your learners need. There are not a lot of materials available that focus on /b/ contrasted with /v/ for example, and this is something you will need if you're teaching in Spain.

2   **Find out about the feature:** Read anything you can find about your chosen feature, and why it may be problematic. Read for example about how /b/ and /v/ are articulated and exactly what the differences between them are. Then try to find out why these two **phonemes** might get confused for **L1** Spanish learners (in Spanish, they are variants of the same phoneme).

3   **Gather a bank of data:** Brainstorm a list of examples of your target feature. Reference material can help here. If you want a list of short words beginning with /b/, you can look under *b* in a dictionary. If you want words beginning with /k/, you'd have to look under both

c and *k*. Finding words with target phonemes in the middle or at the end of words is more difficult – I make great use of rhyming dictionaries for this purpose. If you're looking for **minimal pairs,** try an internet search such as "minimal pairs cot coat".

4   **Scan your data for inspiration:** Stare at your brainstormed list for a while and see if you notice any patterns or topics. If, for example, a number of your words relate to parts of the body, then that could be a theme for a dialogue. The idea you come up with must be feasible for your target feature. For example, you can't make a minimal pair activity to focus on the contrast between /θ/ and /ð/ since there are no pairs for this. You'll need to deal with that in a different way.

5   **Create a prototype:** Make a start to see if your idea has any chance of success. For example, if you want to write a dialogue containing lots of examples of your target feature, write a few lines and see if it's going anywhere.

6   **Check the validity:** At this point, before going on to do a final polished version of your material, check that it focuses on what you want it to focus on. For example, if you want to focus on the **aspiration** of /p/, then the word *sport* is a poor example because it isn't aspirated in this **consonant cluster.** It's always a good idea to try out your material with another teacher if possible, to identify this kind of problem.

7   **Make a final version:** Now you can complete your piece of material to make it classroom ready. Decide if you're going to make printed worksheets or a PowerPoint slide or whatever. You don't have to write teacher's notes if it's just for you, but it may be a good idea – you often discover a problem with it at this stage.

8   **Review:** Although you might not feel like it, do try to make notes on how your material went in class so that you can make improvements to it next time around. One reflection that I find surprisingly frequent is that the activity was too elaborate and too difficult to explain. But once your material works well, share it around the school!

Patsko, L. and Simpson, K. (2019) *How to Write Pronunciation Activities.* ELT Teacher 2 Writer.

> You can help your class to learn, but you can't learn for
> them. Learning is something they must do for themselves,
> so the more autonomy they have, the better.

Have your learners ever asked you what they can do to work on their
pronunciation outside of class? Here are eight suggestions that you
could give them. Have your learners never asked? Why not give them
the tips anyway?

1   **Use self-study materials:** Check out what publishers have available on
    English pronunciation which can be used for self-study. These kinds of
    materials are often accompanied with recorded audio support material
    online. Remember that not all books about pronunciation are suitable:
    some are written for language teachers rather than learners.

2   **Get familiar with phonemic symbols:** There are pros and cons about
    using the symbols in class (see Tip 20), but for self-study, I think the
    arguments must be in favour. The symbols are empowering: they
    provide a kind of vocabulary not only to talk about sounds, but also
    to simply *think* clearly about them. Plus, familiarity with symbols will
    enable learners to use more of the self-study materials that are available.

3   **Exploit dictionaries:** Learner dictionaries have transcriptions of the
    words, including their grammatical variants, and stress markings.
    Although learners can listen to the pronunciation of words using
    the search engines on their phones, that doesn't guarantee a reliable
    result. It's easy to persist in a mispronunciation despite having heard
    the word; seeing the written transcription helps to fix it in the mind
    more accurately.

4   **Record yourself:** Nobody likes the sound of their own recorded
    voice, but it's worth getting used to it. You'll find that you can
    work out for yourself most of what's wrong and right about your
    pronunciation when you listen. It also gives you a lasting record of
    your progress.

5   Use **online videos:** You can get online videos of people talking, such as TED talks, and use them to study pronunciation. Often you can get the transcript as subtitles, which can help. Find a very short segment and play it back over and over, trying to mirror it – copy the voice and gestures. Don't feel that the person needs to be a 'native speaker'. Actually, the most useful would probably be somebody from your own language background who is proficient at English.

6   Use **broadcast resources:** Check out the possibilities of free broadcast materials. For example, there's 'Learning English with CBC' (Canadian Broadcasting Corporation) and 'BBC Learning English' (British Broadcasting Corporation). This latter has some good pronunciation videos.

7   **Be selective about apps:** There are computer programs and phone apps which offer pronunciation practice and guidance. Some are rather unimaginative – the kinds of tasks that if you saw them in a book, you wouldn't buy it. So check before you buy: is it appealing, with a good coverage of pronunciation points? One type of app which is very promising for pronunciation work is voice-recognition technology – see Tip 48 for more on this.

8   Use **English as a Lingua Franca:** The best way to develop your English pronunciation is by using it, and it's worth looking at the possibilities of doing that online with people from other countries. It might be hard to find 'native speakers' for this because they may feel they don't need the practice themselves. The good news, however, is that you can practise English as a Lingua Franca with anybody who speaks English, and that's half the world.

If your learners are not behaving autonomously, you could encourage them in that direction. Instead of asking them to do follow-up homework, get them to do preparatory homework. For example, if you're planning to work on the *ship* versus *sheep* **minimal pair**, ask them to go through a virtual presentation on a website at home before the lesson, and then do pair work to practise it when they get to class. Doing it before, as an integral part of a lesson, makes homework feel less of an optional add on. If your learners do this, they'll learn a bit about the minimal pair, but more importantly, they'll discover new possibilities and get started on the road to autonomy.

Appendices

Appendix 1: Adrian Underhill's phonemic chart

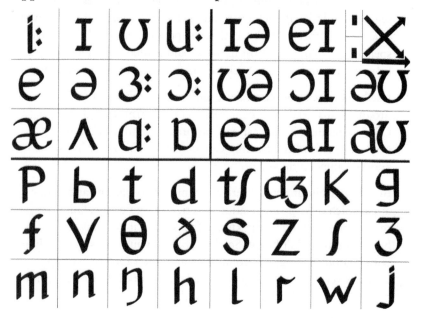

The Original Sound Foundations Phonemic Chart. Copyright Adrian Underhill 2008. Reproduced with permission. Published by Macmillan Education.

Appendix 2: Mark Hancock's *PronPack* vowel chart

IPA Phonemic Symbols as used in British publications

Symbols often used in American publications

Appendix 3: Mouth diagram

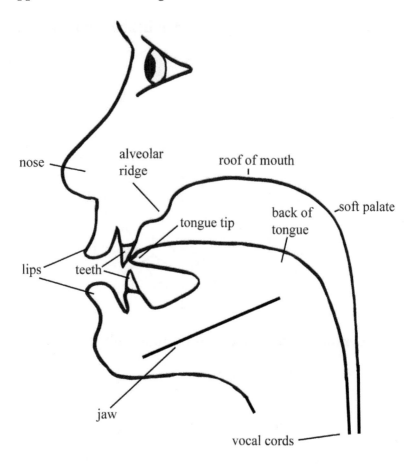

Appendix 4: A pronunciation maze

Go from A to B. Pass through a square only if the word contains the sound /eɪ/.

A eɪ	gave	white	mad	plant	said
have	plane	plan	made	plays	say
please	plain	pack	late	park	plate
hate	rain	what	eight	wash	ways
pays	ran	man	may	maps	paid
wait	weight	states	main	mind	eɪ **B**

Answer key:

gave - plane - plain - rain - hate - pays - wait - weight - states - main - may - eight - late - made - plays - say - plate - ways - paid

Glossary

accent: a way of pronouncing a language which is typical of a specific place or social class, for example, a New York accent, an Indian accent, an upper class accent

accent reduction: a term used, especially in the USA, to describe a type of pronunciation course which has the objective of helping the participant to sound more like a native speaker

accommodation: trying to understand and make yourself understood better to another person, by changing your speech patterns to resemble theirs

alveolar ridge: a bony bump inside the roof of the mouth, just behind the upper teeth

aspiration: the puff of air from the mouth which accompanies the voiceless stop consonants /p/, /t/ and /k/ when they occur at the start of a syllable

assimilation: when one sound is modified so that it sounds more similar to a neighbouring sound

consonant cluster: two or more consonant sounds occurring together

consonants: sounds made when the air stream is blocked or partially blocked by one of the articulators such as the lips, teeth or tongue, as opposed to **vowels**

content words: items of vocabulary which are not simply grammatical. For example, nouns, adjectives and verbs are content words; prepositions, pronouns and auxiliary verbs are not; not **function words**

contrastive stress: stress which a speaker places on a specific word in a sentence to contrast it with something which came up earlier in the discourse

diphthong: a type of vowel phoneme with a distinct change in it – it starts off from one sound but then changes to another

ELF: 'English as a Lingua Franca' – that is, when English is used as a means of communication between people who are not native speakers of English

elision: when a phoneme is cut within a word (for example, the *d* in *sandwich*) or in connected speech (for example, the *d* in *and now*)

elocution: a style of speech which is perceived to be clearer and more correct – nearer to a prestige standard of pronunciation

fricative: a type of consonant in which the air stream is partially but not completely blocked, such as /s/ or /f/

function words: words which serve a grammatical function such as prepositions, pronouns and auxiliary verbs; not **content words**

functional load: how important a pronunciation feature is. For example, the difference between /s/ and /z/ has a high functional load because a lot of words are distinguished by these phonemes. The difference between /θ/ and /ð/ has a low functional load because few words are distinguished by these.

GA: 'General American' – used to refer to a standard form of pronunciation in the USA

glottal stop: a consonant sound in which the air is completely stopped for an instant in the area of the glottis, far down the throat. It commonly replaces the /t/ in words like *button* or phrases like *not now*.

homophones: two words which have a different spelling but the same pronunciation, for example *peace* and *piece*

intrusive sounds: a sound which is inserted to bridge a gap between two other sounds. For example, a /r/ may be inserted between the vowel at the end of *idea* and vowel at the beginning of *of*.

L1: 'first language' – an expression often used to refer to a language learner's mother tongue

lax: a kind of vowel sound in which the mouth muscles are relatively relaxed – as opposed to a **tense** vowel

Lingua Franca Core: a set of pronunciation features which are said to be essential for intelligibility in contexts where people are using English as a Lingua Franca

linking: when two words join together in connected speech so that you can't hear a gap between them

minimal pairs: two words which are identical in pronunciation except for one phoneme, for example *collect* and *correct*

nasals: these are consonant sounds which are created when the air flow is blocked in the mouth but escapes through the nose instead

phoneme: a sound which is recognised as meaningful in a specific language

phonemic symbols: symbols which represent sounds that are recognised as meaningful in a specific language. They appear between slant brackets, for example /e/. There are a range of slightly different sounds which speakers of a language may interpret as being represented by a symbol such as /e/. The symbols found in most language teaching materials are phonemic, not phonetic.

phonetic symbols: symbols which represent possible sounds in all human languages. They appear between square brackets, for example [e], and are intended to represent an exact sound and not a range of sounds. The symbols found in most language teaching materials are phonemic, not phonetic.

phonology: the study of how sounds are used in a language

phonotactics: the study of how sounds may combine in a specific language. For example, an English word cannot begin with the consonant cluster /ps/, but a Greek word can.

pitch: how low or high a note is, both in music and in speech

RP: Received Pronunciation – a standard accent in British English

schwa: a short, indistinct vowel represented by the symbol /ə/ which speakers of English often use in unstressed syllables

soft palate: a part of the roof of the mouth near the back, which is soft rather than bony

stop: a type of consonant sound which involves the air stream being completely blocked for an instant, for example /t/ or /g/

surrender value: how immediately useful something is to learn

target language: the language that a language learner is aiming to learn

tense: a type of vowel which involves a lot of muscle tension around the mouth – as opposed to a **lax** vowel

tone: the aspect of intonation which involves the voice rising or falling in pitch

tonic stress: the aspect of intonation which involves the speaker choosing to put extra emphasis on the most important word in a sentence or phrase

unvoiced: a type of consonant which does not involve vibration of the vocal cords – as opposed to **voiced**. Also known as 'voiceless'.

voice settings: the neutral starting position of the mouth for a specific language. For example, the voice settings for a native speaker of French are different from those of a native speaker of English. Also known as 'articulatory settings'.

voiced: a type of consonant which involves vibration of the vocal cords – as opposed to **unvoiced**

vowel digraphs: relating to spelling – where two vowel letters occur next to each other. For example, the word *read* contains the vowel digraph *ea*.

vowels: a type of sound which is made when the air stream is not obstructed by one of the articulators such as the lips, teeth or tongue – as opposed to **consonants**

weak forms: an alternative form of a function word such as an auxiliary verb, pronoun or connector when it is unstressed in connected speech. Very often, the vowel in a weak form is a schwa, and there may be elision of consonants.

word stress: in words which have more than one syllable, one of the syllables is typically said with more force than the others. For example, the word stress in *banana* is on the second syllable.

Index